LIVES IN THE BALANCE

HIGH/SCOPE
EDUCATIONAL RESEARCH FOUNDATION
Ypsilanti, Michigan

*Monographs of the
High/Scope Educational Research Foundation
Number Eleven*

LIVES IN THE BALANCE
Age-27 Benefit-Cost Analysis of the High/Scope Perry Preschool Program

W. Steven Barnett

foreword by
Lawrence J. Schweinhart

THE HIGH/SCOPE PRESS

Published by
High/Scope® Press

A Division of the
High/Scope Educational Research Foundation
600 North River Street
Ypsilanti, Michigan 48198-2898
(313)485-2000, FAX (313)485-0704

Copyright © 1996 by High/Scope Educational Research Foundation. All rights reserved. Except as permitted under the Copyright Act of 1976, no part of this book may be reproduced or distributed in any form or by any means, electronic or mechanical, including photocopy, recording, or any information storage-and-retrieval system, without prior written permission from the publisher. High/Scope is a registered trademark and service mark of the High/Scope Educational Research Foundation.

Marge Senninger, High/Scope Press Editor

Linda Eckel, Cover and Text Design

Library of Congress Cataloging-in-Publication Data

Barnett, W. Steven.
    Lives in the balance : age 27 benefit-cost analysis of the High/Scope Perry Preschool Program / W. Steven Barnett ; foreword by Lawrence J. Schweinhart.
       p.   cm. — (Monographs of the High/Scope Educational Research Foundation ; no. 11)
    Includes bibliographical references (p.   ) and index.
    ISBN 1-57379-007-9
    1. Perry Preschool Project (Ypsilanti, Mich.) —Cost effectiveness—Longitudinal studies. 2. Socially handicapped children—Education—Michigan—Ypsilanti—Cost effectiveness—Longitudinal studies.
3. School children—Michigan—Ypsilanti—Social conditions—Longitudinal studies. 4. Educational surveys—United States.
I. Title. II. Series
LC 4092.M42B35   1996   96-21849
371.96'7'0977435—dc20   CIP

Printed in the United States of America

Contents

Tables and Figures vii

Acknowledgments ix

Foreword xi

I. **Introduction** 2
  The Basis for This Analysis 3
    The Relation to Previous Analyses 4
    The High/Scope Perry Preschool Project 4
      Random assignment 5
      Attrition 6
  The Methodology of the Benefit-Cost Analysis 6
    Define the Scope of the Analysis 7
    Conduct a Cost Analysis 8
    Conduct an Evaluation of Effects 10
    Estimate the Monetary Value of Effects 12
    Adjust for Differences in Dollar Value Over Time,
      and Aggregate 13
      Real dollars 13
      Present value 14
    Describe the Distributional Consequences 15
    Conduct Sensitivity Analyses 15

II. **Estimated Costs and Benefits: Program Costs, Child Care, and Education** 18
  Program Costs 19
    Cost Estimation 19
    Alternative Approaches and a Perspective on Cost 25
  Child Care 27
  Elementary and Secondary Education 28
    Overview 28
    Calculation Procedure 31
  Adult Secondary and Higher Education 35
    Adult Secondary Education 35
    Higher Education 36

III. **Estimated Costs and Benefits: Employment, Crime, and Welfare Assistance** 40
  Employment and Earnings 41
    Earnings Through Age 27 41
    Earnings Beyond Age 27 45
    Other Employment-Related Benefits and Total
      Compensation 48
    Summary of Employment-Related Effects 49

Crime and Delinquency 49
   Benefits Through Age 28 From Crime Reduction 50
      Victim costs 51
      Criminal justice system costs 54
   Crime Costs Beyond Age 28 55
   Summary of Crime Reduction Benefits 55
Welfare 58
   Welfare Costs Through Age 27 58
   Welfare Cost Reductions Beyond Age 27 59
   Summary of Effects on Welfare Payments and Costs to Society 61

IV. **Benefit-Cost Summary and Sensitivity Analyses** 64
Aggregation of Costs and Benefits 65
   Distribution of Costs and Benefits 65
   Gender Differences 68
Sensitivity Analyses 69
   Effect of the Initial Group Difference in Maternal Employment 71
   Alternative Assumptions for Benefit Projections 72
      Crime cost reductions 73
      Welfare cost reductions 73
      Earnings 73
   Omitted Benefits 74
   Alternative Discount Rates 76
   General Robustness With Respect to Changes in Magnitudes of Benefits 77
   Global Effects 81
Generalizing From This Benefit-Cost Analysis 83

V. **Public Policy Implications** 84
Research Supporting High/Scope Perry Preschool Project Findings 85
The Potential of Preschool Programs Today 87
   The Population Served 87
   Program Quality 88
   Program Quantity 88
   The Broader Environment 89
The Need for Further Research 89
Ignoring the Evidence—-What Are the Costs? 90

Appendix 93

References 95

Index 101

Tables and Figures

Tables

1. Number of High/Scope Perry Preschool Study Participants by Group and Wave 5
2. Potential Costs and Benefits of the High/Scope Perry Preschool Program 9
3. Preschool Program Effects Related to Economic Benefits 11
4. Costs of the High/Scope Perry Preschool Program in Each Year's Current Dollars 20
5. Instructional Staff Costs (in Each Year's Current Dollars) 21
6. Special Services Administrative and Support Staff Costs (in Each Year's Current Dollars) 22
7. School District Overhead Costs (in Each Year's Current Dollars) 22
8. Program Group's Share of Screening Costs (in Each Year's Current Dollars) 23
9. Distribution of Fixed Capital of Ypsilanti Public School District 24
10. Calculation of Implicit Interest and Depreciation (in Each Year's Current Dollars) 25
11. Education Costs per Child-Year by Program Category (in Constant 1981 Dollars) 33
12. Education Costs per Child-Year, Including Estimated Years (in Constant 1981 Dollars) 34
13. Estimated Effects of the High/Scope Perry Preschool Program on Elementary and Secondary Education Cost per Child (in Real 1992 Dollars) 35
14. Estimated Costs of Higher Education at 2- and 4-Year Public Institutions Between 1976 and 1991 (in Real 1992 Dollars) 37
15. Estimated Effects of the High/Scope Perry Preschool Program on Higher Education Cost per Person (in Real 1992 Dollars) 38
16. Estimated Mean Annual Earnings at Ages 16 Through 19 and Ages 25 Through 27 by Group and Gender (in Real 1992 Dollars) 43
17. Projected Lifetime Earnings Beyond Age 27 (in Real 1992 Dollars) 47
18. Estimated Projected (Age 28–65) Program Effects on per Person Earnings of Program Participants (in Real 1992 Dollars) 47
19. Program Effects on per Person Lifetime Earnings and Total Compensation (in Real 1992 Dollars) 49
20. Victim Costs by Type of Crime (in Real 1992 Dollars) 52
21. Estimated Victim Costs by Component (in Real 1985 Dollars) 53
22. Estimated Criminal Justice System Costs (Excluding Corrections) by Type of Crime (in Real 1992 Dollars) 54
23. Estimated per Person Crime Costs by Program Attendance and Gender (in Real 1992 Dollars) 56
24. Preschool Program's Estimated per Person Crime Cost Reductions (in Real 1992 Dollars) 56
25. Present Value of Estimated per Person Crime Cost Reductions (in Real 1992 Dollars) 57
26. Estimated per Person Welfare Payments by Program Attendance and Gender (in Real 1992 Dollars, Undiscounted) 61
27. Present Value of Estimated Preschool Program Effect on Welfare Payments (in Real 1992 Dollars) 62
28. Preschool Program's Estimated Effects per Program Participant (Present Value, 1992 Dollars Discounted at 3%) 66

29 Preschool Program's Estimated Effects per Female Program Participant (Present Value, 1992 Dollars Discounted at 3%) 69

30 Preschool Program's Estimated Effects per Male Program Participant (Present Value, 1992 Dollars Discounted at 3%) 70

31 Preschool Program's Estimated Effects per Program Participant (Present Value, 1992 Dollars Discounted at 5%) 77

32 Preschool Program's Estimated Effects per Program Participant (Present Value, 1992 Dollars Discounted at 7%) 78

33 Preschool Program's Estimated Effects per Program Participant (Present Value, 1992 Dollars Discounted at 9%) 79

34 Preschool Program's Estimated Effects per Program Participant (Present Value, 1992 Dollars Discounted at 10%) 80

35 Preschool Program's Estimated Effects per Program Participant (Present Value, 1992 Dollars Discounted at 11%) 81

A1 Correlations Between Program Outcomes and Mother Employed at Study Entry 93

Figures

1 Return to Taxpayers on per Participant Investmant xii

2 Costs and Benefits for Society per Preschool Program Participant 86

Acknowledgments

My work on this monograph has benefited from the assistance of many others. Deborah Jewett was invaluable as a research assistant. Gerry Musgrave provided advice on data sources and on economics, as well as encouragement whenever it was needed.

An author is fortunate to have a good editor, and in this work I was doubly blessed. Marge Senninger and Lawrence Schweinhart both edited the manuscript with great skill. My discussions with Lawrence Schweinhart about the High/Scope Perry Preschool program and its effects now extend over 15 years, and his contributions have become so integrated with my own work that they are difficult to identify and impossible to enumerate. Unquestionably, this monograph was much improved by his efforts.

Finally, like all benefit-cost analyses, this one owes a great deal to the quality of the underlying study. That quality is due to David Weikart, Lawrence Schweinhart, and the many others who have worked at High/Scope under their leadership. David Weikart founded the High/Scope Educational Research Foundation and initiated the High/Scope Perry Preschool Project, a study that has continued for over three decades. Few studies can rival the High/Scope Perry Preschool study, and we are fortunate that the project's initiator, like pioneers in another field in the 1960s, had "the right stuff."

Foreword

By translating the long-term evaluation of a preschool program into the language of business and public policy, benefit-cost analysis of the High/Scope Perry Preschool program has played an important role in shaping early childhood program policy at the end of the twentieth century.

The High/Scope Perry Preschool program was remarkably effective. The evidence through program participants' early adulthood indicates that it reduced their need for special school services, increased their earnings and property wealth, reduced their dependency on welfare assistance, and cut their crime rate in half (Schweinhart, Barnes, & Weikart, 1993). The program's effectiveness would have gone unrecognized, however, had it not been subject to an internally valid, scientific evaluation that followed participants for some 22 years after they completed the program. Indeed, for lack of such scientific evaluation, programs of equal or greater effectiveness may exist today without anyone knowing how beneficial they are.

This benefit-cost analysis, conducted at the point when program participants were 27 years old, is a definitive economic summary of the High/Scope Perry Preschool study. It compares the dollar cost of providing the High/Scope Perry Preschool program with the dollar value of its various benefits, as shown in Figure 1 on the next page.

In 1992 constant dollars discounted at 3% annually, the program cost $12,356 per participant to operate ($7,252 per child per school year, with 13 children attending 1 year and 45 attending 2 years). Offsetting this investment were the following average per participant returns to the taxpayers: a $6,287 return due to the participant's decreased overall schooling costs, an $8,847 return from increased taxes paid on the participant's higher earnings, a $2,918 return due to the reduced cost of welfare assistance to the participant, a $12,796 return due to decreased justice-system costs, and a $57,585 return due to decreased crime-victim costs. Thus, the $12,356 investment per participant provided a total return to taxpayers of $88,433, which is $7.16 for every dollar invested. This clearly provides policymakers with a sound basis for the decision to invest in preschool programs — if they can be implemented on the scale needed and at the same time hold to the standards of quality set by the High/Scope Perry Preschool program.

Knowledge of the High/Scope Perry program's return on public investment has affected how U. S. business leaders and policymakers think about preschool programs. The Committee for Economic Development — a group of 200 chief executive officers of the nation's leading corporations and universities — has thrown its weight behind public investment in high-quality preschool programs, publishing several books on the topic (Research and Policy Committee of the Committee for Economic Development, 1985, 1987) and persuading individual state and federal policymakers to take action. As a result, the states investing in preschool programs have increased from 7 in 1980 (Mitchell, Seligson, & Marx, 1989) to 32 in 1992, with those 32 states spending $665 million to serve almost 290,000 children (Adams & Sandfort, 1994). Furthermore, with bipartisan congressional support spearheaded first by President Bush and then by President

Figure 1
RETURN TO TAXPAYERS ON
PER PARTICIPANT INVESTMENT

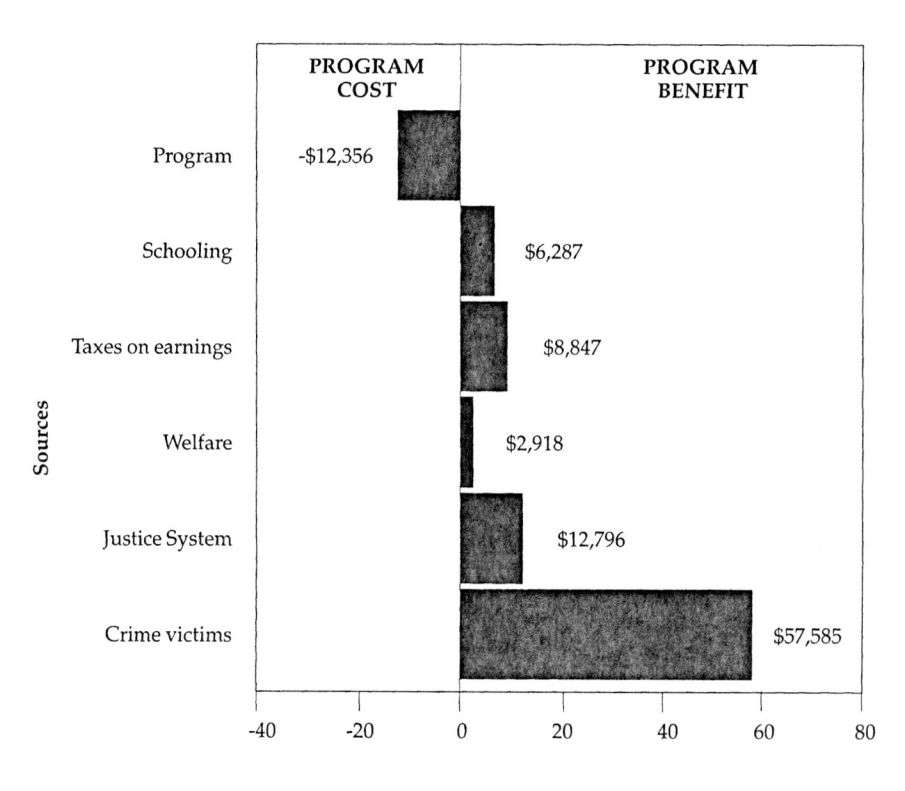

Sources	PROGRAM COST	PROGRAM BENEFIT
Program	-$12,356	
Schooling		$6,287
Taxes on earnings		$8,847
Welfare		$2,918
Justice System		$12,796
Crime victims		$57,585

Present Value in Thousands (1992 $ Discounted at 3%)

Total public benefits: $88,433   Net public benefits: $76,077   Return on the dollar: $7.16

Note: From *Significant Benefits* (p.168), by L. J. Schweinhart et al., 1993, Ypsilanti, MI: High/Scope Press. Copyright 1993 by High/Scope Educational Research Foundation.

Clinton, federal spending for Head Start increased from $1.2 billion in 1988 to $3.5 billion in 1995 (U.S. Administration on Children, Youth and Families, 1995). Looking beyond the United States, we find other signs of increased interest in preschool programs: The World Bank, for example, recently adopted early childhood development programs as a focus of its investment in Third World countries.

In addition to increasing spending on preschool programs, policymakers have focused attention on improving preschool program quality, which is essential to producing the desired benefits. States have defined standards for quality in the early childhood programs they fund. And Congress has in recent years earmarked funding specifically for Head Start quality improvement; both the federal Head Start Bureau and the National Head Start Association have emphasized the quality issue as well. In 1996, the Administration on Children, Youth and Families, for example, initiated a 5-year, $10 million Head Start Quality Research Consortium of four centers, including one at the High/Scope Educational Research Foundation, to develop Head Start Performance Measures and to focus on issues of quality in Head Start.

Taking a cue from the movie *It's a Wonderful Life,* we can think about what the world would have been like without the longitudinal High/Scope Perry Preschool study and its benefit-cost analysis. It is easy to imagine Head Start having fallen to David Stockman's budget axe in the early days of the Reagan Administration. Or we might envision, in more recent times, program funding leveling out and being gradually reduced to help balance the federal budget. State funding of preschool programs could to this day have remained limited to a handful of states, as it was in 1980. Those states might even have dropped their preschool programs by now, in favor of funding massive prison expansion.

Certainly, the benefit-cost analysis of the High/Scope Perry Preschool program does not stand alone in supporting high-quality preschool programs for young children living in poverty. Many studies demonstrate the short-term effectiveness of such programs, and half a dozen studies identify key long-term benefits (Schweinhart et al., 1993). But it can properly be said that the High/Scope work has crystalized the message of these studies, serving as a rallying point for policymakers. Scientific hypotheses do not stand or fall on the basis of any single study, even a single study of unusual complexity and uniqueness. In the long run, the findings of the High/Scope Perry Preschool study beg for confirmation from similar studies. In the meantime, they serve as the best evidence of the extraordinary potential of high-quality preschool programs for young children living in poverty.

Lawrence J. Schweinhart

LIVES IN THE BALANCE

I Introduction

This monograph explains the methodology and findings of the benefit-cost analysis of the High/Scope Perry Preschool program and its long-term effects on participants. The explanation should be useful to those who wish to understand not only the social impact of the High/Scope Perry Preschool program but also the impact of early childhood education in general. The High/Scope Perry Preschool Project, which is the study documenting the effects of the High/Scope Perry Preschool program in Ypsilanti, Michigan, is noted for providing the most complete longitudinal data available on the long-term effects of a preschool program on children from economically disadvantaged families. The most recent description of this study and its results was presented by Schweinhart, Barnes, and Weikart (1993).

The benefit-cost analysis described here is an example of the practical application of economic analysis to research on early childhood programs. In the field of early childhood care and education, economic analyses are relatively rare compared to efficacy studies, and most attempts at economic analysis of early childhood programs have been methodologically inadequate (Barnett & Escobar, 1987, 1990). We hope that this monograph will contribute to a better understanding of the methodological requirements of benefit-cost analysis and how it might be applied to other early childhood programs.

The Basis for This Analysis

Benefit-cost analysis is a tool for economic evaluation of policies or programs. Essentially, it is a means of measuring and comparing the disadvantages (costs) and advantages (benefits) of a program. Benefit-cost analysis allows one to estimate the net gain to society as a whole and to examine the distribution of gains and losses among society's members. The benefit-cost analysis presented here was designed to address two questions:

- First, was the High/Scope Perry Preschool program a profitable investment for the society that sponsored it, that is, did its benefits exceed its costs?

- Second, what was the distribution of costs and benefits between the general public, or taxpayers who paid for the program, and program participants?

The basic rationale for benefit-cost analysis is that better decisions about policy and practice can be made if society's members know the economic impact of a policy or program. The benefits and costs of the High/Scope Perry Preschool program — a specific program with particular people at a given historical moment — are of interest to policymakers inasmuch as they shed light on the likely economic return and distribution of costs and benefits from similar programs now and in the future. Therefore, generalization of the findings of this analysis is an important issue addressed in the design of the analysis and throughout this monograph.

The Relation to Previous Analyses

Benefit-cost analysis has been a part of the High/Scope Perry Preschool Project for many years. Extensive economic analyses were conducted at two earlier points — first, when data were available from the age-10 follow-up study (Weber, Foster, & Weikart, 1978), and then, at the time of the next major follow-up study, which collected data through age 19 (Barnett, 1985a, 1985b; Berrueta-Clement, Schweinhart, Barnett, Epstein, & Weikart, 1984). The benefit-cost analysis presented here builds directly on the age-19 analysis. It incorporates estimates from the age-19 analysis (Barnett, 1985b) where appropriate and provides new estimates where new data from the age-27 follow-up are applicable. The methods and findings of this analysis have been summarized in a brief report (Barnett, 1993a) and published in greater detail as part of the age-27 monograph (Barnett, 1993b). The report presented here is an even more comprehensive explanation of those same methods and results.

In the previous analyses, to estimate benefits over the entire lifetime of the participants, some future benefits had to be projected based on the data available at the time. In a similar way, this latest benefit-cost analysis makes projections beyond the benefit-cost estimates that are based on actual experience through age 27. However, it is notable that obtaining the age-27 data has at last eliminated the need to rely on future projections to establish the preschool program's profitability. The High/Scope Perry Preschool program has proved to be a sound investment based on benefits obtained by age 27 alone.

The High/Scope Perry Preschool Project

A benefit-cost analysis typically builds on an underlying evaluation that describes a program or policy and estimates its effects. The economic analysis can be no stronger than the evaluation on which it is based. In this case, because of its solid experimental design, long-term follow-up, extraordinarily wide range of potential outcomes examined, and lack of attrition, the evaluation of the High/Scope Perry Preschool program provides an unusually strong basis for a benefit-cost analysis. This monograph provides only a rudimentary description of the program and of High/Scope's long-term study. Further details are available in Schweinhart et al. (1993) and in earlier High/Scope monographs on the High/Scope Perry Preschool Project (Berrueta-Clement et al., 1984; Schweinhart & Weikart, 1980; Weikart, Bond, & McNeil, 1978; Weikart, Deloria, Lawser, & Wiegerink, 1970).

The High/Scope Perry Preschool program was developed along with a plan to study the effects of preschool program participation on children's subsequent school success. The program consisted of 20 to 25 children participating in a 2½-hour classroom session with 4 teachers each weekday morning and each parent and preschooler having a weekly 1½-hour home visit. The Ypsilanti Public School District provided the program at Perry Elementary School for 30 weeks each year from October to May. Classroom staff were certified public school teachers. The curriculum was not entirely consistent over the years but began as a fairly traditional nursery-school

Table 1

NUMBER OF HIGH/SCOPE PERRY PRESCHOOL STUDY
PARTICIPANTS BY GROUP AND WAVE

Wave	Year	Program Group	No-Program Group	Total
Zero	1962	13	15	28
One	1962	8	9	17
Two	1963	12	14	26
Three	1964	13	14	27
Four	1965	12	13	25
All	—	58	65	123

approach and gradually evolved to an explicitly Piagetian approach. Despite this evolution, there was more consistency across the years in the High/Scope Perry Preschool program than would be found in a representative sample of Head Start or public school prekindergarten programs.

The High/Scope Perry Preschool Project began in 1962 with the induction of the first two waves of children — Wave Zero and Wave One — into the study. To achieve mixed-age grouping in the classroom, Wave Zero consisted of 4-year-olds born in 1958, and Wave One consisted of 3-year-olds born in 1959. In each of the next 3 years, another wave of 3-year-olds entered the study. A total of 128 low-socioeconomic-status African-American children from a single school-attendance area in Ypsilanti, Michigan, entered the study over these 4 years. Five children were lost to the study because they moved away shortly after study entry or died during the preschool years, so the sample for follow-up was composed of 123 children. Table 1 displays the distribution of the final sample by group and wave.

Random assignment. Study participants were randomly assigned to program and no-program groups, with two minor exceptions. First, when the study encountered younger siblings of children who had entered the study in previous waves (only 100 different families were represented in the original sample of 128 children), the younger sibling was assigned to the same group (program or no-program) as the older sibling. Otherwise some children in the no-program group would have been exposed to the influence of older siblings who had attended the classes and parents who had received the home visits, and the comparison would have been weakened. Second, after the random assignments, 2 children were shifted from the program to the no-program group because their mothers' hours of employment prevented them from attending the preschool classes or participating in the home visits.

As a result of the random assignment, the two groups did not differ at project entry to a statistically significant extent (at $p < .05$, two-tailed) on Stanford-Binet IQ (Terman & Merrill, 1960), family socioeconomic status, mother's or father's highest year of schooling, number of children in the family, number of siblings older or younger than the study participant, child's age, mother's and father's age, rooms in home, or persons per room at study entry; neither were the two groups significantly different in percentages of males and females, family configuration (single-parent vs. two-parent, nuclear vs. extended), father's employment level, family welfare status, family in public housing, geographic region or population of mother's birthplace, or family religion. Children in the program group did have significantly fewer mothers in paid employment than did those in the no-program group (9% vs. 31%), a difference partly due to the transfer of 2 children from the program group to the no-program group, as described in the previous paragraph. Statistical analysis found that this difference introduced a negligible bias that tended to result in the *underestimation* of program benefits (see Sensitivity Analyses on p. 69).

Attrition. Attrition, the loss of subjects after a study begins, can be a source of major difficulties in longitudinal studies. Attrition can negatively affect a study by so severely reducing the number of participants for whom there are data that it is impossible to obtain reasonably precise estimates. If it is nonrandom, attrition can result in bias. Attrition can occur for a variety of reasons: One or more subjects might refuse to take a test or interview or simply not respond to particular questions; researchers might be denied access to official records or be unable to locate some participants. Because considerable effort was devoted to avoiding attrition in the High/Scope Perry Preschool study, attrition presented no serious difficulties for the benefit-cost analysis. Attrition was low throughout the study, with a median of 4.9% and a mean of 8.7% across all times and measures (Schweinhart et al., 1993). At the age-27 follow-up, 117 of the 121 participants who were still living completed interviews, and official-records data were reviewed for all 123 participants. Attrition can be ruled out as a source of bias because it was not significantly different between program and no-program groups and did not cause groups to vary significantly from their entry characteristics (Berrueta-Clement et al., 1984; Schweinhart & Weikart, 1980).

The Methodology of the Benefit-Cost Analysis

Our analysis of the High/Scope Perry Preschool program employed standard procedures for benefit-cost analysis. Detailed explanations of these procedures can be found in any number of texts on the application of economic analysis to program evaluation (Gramlich, 1981; Just, Hueth, & Schmitz, 1982; Mishan, 1976; Thompson, 1980). Seven steps are involved:

1. Define the scope of the analysis.
2. Conduct a cost analysis.
3. Conduct an evaluation of effects.
4. Estimate the monetary value of effects.
5. Adjust for differences in dollar value over time, and aggregate.
6. Describe the distributional consequences.
7. Conduct sensitivity analyses.

This section of the monograph briefly explains each of these steps and how it was carried out for this benefit-cost analysis.

Define the Scope of the Analysis

Like all evaluation activities, benefit-cost analysis involves comparison of alternatives. The first step in planning this analysis was to define the alternatives to be evaluated and the bounds of the evaluation, in order to decide whose costs and benefits to count and what program outcomes to examine. The analysis is intended to inform researchers and policymakers interested in generalizing as broadly as possible about the costs and benefits of preschool education. We therefore defined the alternatives and the bounds of the evaluation with that intent in mind.

The alternatives compared are preschool education and no preschool education. The experimental design of the High/Scope Perry Preschool study nicely sets up the comparison so one need only compare the average for the program group to the average for the no-program group to estimate the preschool program's cost or benefit per child. The comparison is slightly complicated by two factors. One is that some children had 1 year of the preschool program, whereas others had 2 years. The other is that the percentages of males and females in the study were not equal. The procedures followed with respect to both of these complications took into account the likely use of this benefit-cost analysis to make inferences about public policy.

This analysis presents benefit and cost estimates only for the High/Scope Perry program as a whole. The first benefit-cost analysis (based on data through age 10) calculated separate estimates for children who attended 1 year and children who attended 2 years (Weber et al., 1978). However, the small number of children attending only 1 year resulted in benefit estimates for the 1-year group that lacked reliability; this left the 2-year benefit estimates as a basis for policymaking. The second benefit-cost analysis (based on age-19 data) produced separate cost estimates for 1-year and 2-year attendance, but only one set of benefit estimates based on the entire sample (Barnett, 1985a). The advantage of this latter approach was that it increased the reliability of the benefit estimates by basing them on the full sample. Although the researchers cautioned that this did not imply that similar benefits could be obtained from either 1 or 2 years of the preschool program, some confusion about this matter seems to have resulted.

The basic difficulty researchers faced was this: Because only 13 children attended the preschool program for just 1 year, while the remaining 45 program-group children attended for 2 years, the High/Scope Perry Preschool study could provide only limited evidence about the effects of 1-year versus 2-year attendance. The small number attending for 1 year severely limited the study's power to detect differences in effects between 1 and 2 years, so this absence of statistically significant differences for those attending 1 year versus 2 years was not highly informative. (To be statistically significant, differences between 1-year and 2-year effects would have to be as large as 50 percentage points.) However, limiting the analysis to just those children who had 2 years of the preschool program would have reduced an already-small sample size by 22%.

This benefit-cost analysis sought to produce the most reliable estimates possible and to provide a valid comparison for policymakers by combining data from all waves to estimate costs and benefits. This produced estimates that are weighted averages for a preschool program that was attended for 1 year by 22% of the children and for 2 years by 78% of the children. Serendipitously, this may be reasonably close to the 1- and 2-year attendance patterns that would result if 2 years of public preschool education were made available to all low-income families through Head Start or the public schools (Hofferth, West, Henke, & Kaufman, 1994). In interpreting the benefit-cost analysis results, it should be kept in mind that having all children attend a 1-year preschool program would cost roughly half as much as having all children attend a 2-year program but would not necessarily produce the same benefits as a 2-year program. Furthermore, a 2-year program with *all* children attending both years would cost only slightly more than the High/Scope Perry Preschool program cost but might have somewhat greater benefits because all the children attended for 2 years.

The other feature of this benefit-cost analysis that policymakers should note is that although the High/Scope Perry Preschool study sample had more males than females (59% vs. 41%), benefit-cost estimates were calculated so they represent results for a population with equal numbers of males and females. To do this, first all benefits were estimated separately for males and females, and then these separate estimates were weighted equally to produce an average for the general population. Otherwise, whenever benefits from the preschool program differed for males and females, the imbalance in the sample could have had a significant impact on the results, producing estimates less accurate for the population as a whole. As it turns out, the estimated value of all lifetime benefits is virtually identical for males and females. Therefore, this feature of the analysis has no effect on the overall results. However, there are large differences between males and females for some specific types of benefits.

We decided to examine the total costs and benefits to society as a whole and to divide these into those accruing to taxpayers and those accruing specifically to program participants and their families. All effects were to be included, whether intended or unintended. Table 2 presents an outline of potential costs and benefits based on previous research and economic theory. As can be seen, education has been found to be related to a wide variety of social and economic outcomes for adolescents and adults (Haveman & Wolfe, 1984). Of course, because of measurement and design limitations, not all of the potential effects in Table 2 could be evaluated.

Conduct a Cost Analysis

Our estimate of the cost of the program to taxpayers was based on information describing the program and on historical data on program expenditures. An ingredients approach to cost analysis was used to identify and estimate the costs of all resources used by the preschool program — operating costs, capital costs, and administrative costs associated with the school district in which it was located. Cost was estimated using the actual historical prices

Table 2

POTENTIAL COSTS AND BENEFITS
OF THE HIGH/SCOPE PERRY PRESCHOOL PROGRAM

Costs

Costs of preschool program

Taxpayers' costs of providing program

Participants' out-of-pocket costs—transportation, school supplies, school clothes

Parents' opportunity costs—time required for transportation, home visits, and parent meetings

Children's opportunity costs—activities missed while in the preschool program

Costs of later education and related services

Taxpayers' costs of providing programs

Participants' out-of-pocket costs (e.g., college tuition)

Participants' opportunity costs (e.g., foregone earnings and leisure of those who continue education longer)

Benefits (*to the children who attended the preschool program*)

From increased human capital (investment benefits)

Educational success and satisfaction

Earnings and fringe benefits in the labor force

Earnings in the underground economy

Productivity in household activities

Nonlabor income

Accumulation of capital goods and wealth

Occupational and social status

Value of leisure

Quality of social, especially family, relationships

Control over timing and frequency of childbearing

Benefits to their children from improved parenting and greater family resources

From immediate preschool program experience

Enjoyment and enrichment of program

Results of services child was referred to by the preschool program

Benefits (*to parents of children who attended the preschool program*)

Child care provision

Home visits and social activities

Satisfaction derived from preschool program experiences and results for their children

Table 2 continues on next page

Table 2 (continued)

POTENTIAL COSTS AND BENEFITS
OF THE HIGH/SCOPE PERRY PRESCHOOL PROGRAM

Benefits (*to siblings of children who attended the preschool program*)

    Direct effects of preschool program on parenting skills and parents' interactions with their children

    Effects on sibling interaction (e.g., older siblings teaching younger what they have learned)

    Indirect effects of preschool program on parents who may seek to compensate the child who did not receive the benefit of the program

---

Benefits (*to taxpayers*)

    Decreased costs of government expenditures
        Education
        Social services
        Criminal justice system

    Increased tax revenues paid by program participants

    Increased societal equity

    Decreased social problems
        Crime and delinquency
        Teenage pregnancy

    Increased citizen competence and participation

(including teacher salaries) rather than current salaries and benefits. This was consistent with the procedure used to estimate benefits. All cost figures were adjusted to 1992 dollars to make them comparable across years and more meaningful to audiences in the mid-1990s. Estimation of the cost of the preschool program is fully discussed in Chapter 2 of this monograph.

Conduct an Evaluation of Effects

The benefit-cost analysis depends completely on the underlying evaluation of the effects of the program. The High/Scope Perry Preschool study's design provided a strong basis for estimating these effects, including an extremely broad range of data collected on children and their families before, during, and after the program. Data on the children were collected continuously during their elementary school years, and then at ages 14–15, 19, and 27. These data allowed for a comparison of the program group with the no-program group on many (though not all) of the costs and benefits listed in Table 2.

The evaluation of the High/Scope Perry Preschool program found a chain of effects stretching from the preschool years into the school years

Table 3

PRESCHOOL PROGRAM EFFECTS RELATED TO ECONOMIC BENEFITS

Outcome Variables	Program Group Measure	N	No-Program Group Measure	N
Education effects				
California Achievement Test at Age 14 (mean raw score)	122.2	49	94.5	46
Ever classified as mentally impaired	15%	54	35%	58
Graduated from high school by age 19	66%	58	45%	65
Employment effects				
Employed at age 19	50%	58	32%	63
Mean monthly earnings at age 27	$1,219	54	$766	61
Homeowner at age 27	36%	56	13%	61
Owner of two cars at age 27	30%	56	13%	61
Crime effects				
Arrested by age 19	31%	58	51%	63
5 or more arrests through age 28	7%	58	35%	63
Welfare effects				
Received welfare at age 19	18%	58	32%	63
Received welfare through age 27	59%	58	80%	63

Note. All group differences are statistically significant at the .05 level.

and then into adulthood. Table 3 presents a list of important effects from the standpoint of the economic analysis. Identifying the links in the causal chain explaining how the preschool program produced these effects is a difficult process and one about which there are sure to be disagreements. However, confidence in the benefit-cost analysis does not depend on a complete causal model linking all effects from beginning to end. Rather, the strength of the experimental design is sufficient assurance that the estimated effects are due to the program and due to a small number of causal links (e.g., between educational attainment and earnings) that are well established by economic theory and empirical research.

Unavoidably, some of the underlying effects listed in Table 2 could not be estimated from the available data and so could not be included in the economic analysis. Although the omissions were not extensive enough to pose serious threats to the overall validity of the results, some of them do warrant discussion. The most common reason that some benefits in Table 2 were unassessed is that the High/Scope Perry Preschool study provides no data for estimating potential effects on the program participants' family members, neighbors, or fellow students. Of these, effects on siblings may be the most important. At least one study of early intervention for disadvantaged children has found evidence of substantial effects on siblings (Seitz & Apfel, 1994).

As indicated in Table 2, parents' interactions with *all* their children could have been altered by what they learned from the home visits or as a result of one child's participation in the preschool program. For example, children who attended the preschool program might have requested that parents read to them more often, and home visits might have increased reading to other children as well. Children who attended the preschool program might have affected their siblings through direct interactions or by serving as role models. Finally, when one child attended the preschool program, parents might have redirected resources (including their own time) toward other children in the family. For example, having one child attend the preschool program may have allowed a mother at home to devote more attention to younger siblings for several hours a day. In addition, some parents, wanting to equalize the resources going to their children, might have reasoned that if one child attended the program, fairness demanded that the others get some other advantage.

Another omission from the economic analysis (and from Table 2) concerns global or spillover effects on the school and neighborhood. A preschool program provided on a large scale, available to all or a large percentage of children in a neighborhood, could significantly change the social climate of a neighborhood or a school. It could also create bandwagon effects due to changes in peer-group norms about what is acceptable or desirable behavior. Such effects may simply not occur as the result of a small-scale program, like the High/Scope Perry Preschool program, in which only a few children in a school or neighborhood are affected.

If anything, the exclusion of sibling and spillover effects from the economic analysis seems likely to bias the results toward underestimation of the benefits from the preschool program. However, there is another type of effect that might produce bias in the direction of overestimation. What is called "queuing bias" would occur if benefits for those in the program group were gained at the expense of other persons by bumping them out of line for some benefit. For example, one estimated benefit from the preschool program is a reduction in special education placements and their costs. However, if the school system's special education programs still served the same total number of students, replacing special education candidates from the preschool program with other special education candidates, then the system's costs for special education might not have decreased as a result of the preschool program. Similarly, if the program group increased its employment by taking jobs away from others, the net increase in earnings from employment would be much less than estimated. There is no way to estimate queuing bias from the information the study provides. Whether or not one believes that queuing bias is a serious threat to the results of this analysis depends on whether one believes life to be a zero-sum game in which one person's gain requires another's loss.

Estimate the Monetary Value of Effects

Estimation of the monetary value of program effects is the defining characteristic of benefit-cost analysis. This step puts all program effects, all costs and benefits, on an equal footing by translating them into dollars. This allows the analyst to aggregate costs and benefits to produce a single measure of the program's economic impact on society and to investigate the distribution of costs and benefits among various groups within society (taxpayers and participants, in this case). Inevitably this step is accomplished imperfectly and incompletely. Some documented effects are difficult to valuate monetarily; as indicated earlier, some likely effects are not even documented. Yet, if the benefit-cost analysis is to be useful, the analyst must produce credible estimates of the monetary value of a substantial portion of the program's effects.

Despite the difficulties of moving from the potential effects in Table 2 and the documented effects in Table 3 to dollar estimates of costs and benefits, this analysis encompassed enough of the important benefits of the High/Scope Perry Preschool program to provide a useful assessment of the preschool program's economic impact on society. The economic value of benefits was estimated for seven major benefit categories: (1) child care, (2) regular elementary and secondary education, (3) adult secondary education, (4) higher education, (5) delinquency and crime, (6) earnings and employment, and (7) welfare (public assistance).

Certain likely effects of the High/Scope Perry preschool program go well beyond those for which economic benefits can be estimated. The program could have resulted in improvements in the quality of household production, leisure, and family relationships; intrinsic and personal rewards of school success and increased satisfaction with school; increased control over reproduction, including avoidance of out-of-wedlock pregnancy and decreased reliance on abortion; and increased social standing and personal sense of accomplishment relating to greater economic success and lower involvement in delinquency and crime. Though these effects may have been valuable to the program participants and their families, no satisfactory way of estimating their monetary value was identified.

Adjust for Differences in Dollar Value Over time, and Aggregate

In analyses like this one in which costs and benefits span more than one year, dollar values from different years must be adjusted to make them comparable. One adjustment is made to remove the effects of inflation and translate nominal dollars from each year of the study into dollars of one given year, that is, dollars of equal purchasing power, or *real dollars.* An additional adjustment takes into account the time value of money by calculating the *present value* of real dollars from a given year. The two adjustments can be explained as follows:

Real dollars. For all of the years in which data were collected (through age 27), a real-dollar cost or benefit in any given year reflects the effects of inflation (i.e., it takes into account that a dollar in 1965, near the beginning of the project, would buy considerably more than a dollar in 1990). We have adjusted all nominal dollars for costs or benefits through age 27 to allow for inflation. This was done by using a Gross Domestic Product (GDP) implicit price deflator to convert nominal dollars from various years into *real dollars* (dollars having the same purchasing power) in a single year. For ease of reference, we converted all costs and benefits to 1992 dollars.

Present value. In addition to adjusting dollars for inflation, it is necessary to calculate their *present value,* to account for the time value, or "opportunity cost," of money. Even in the absence of inflation, a dollar received now is more valuable than a dollar received some time in the future, because the dollar in hand can be used this year. It can be invested in a productive enterprise to yield a positive return over and above inflation, or it can be used to purchase a consumer good that can be enjoyed over the year. To account for time value, we equalize the values of real dollars (inflation-adjusted dollars) by using a *real discount rate* constant across all years (as opposed to a nominal, or money, rate, which includes an inflation factor that varies from year to year). This real discount rate is used to calculate *present value* — the value of a dollar from a given year expressed in terms of the value of a dollar at the beginning of the program or policy (the first year). In this case, the "first year" is defined as the year of a cohort's study entry (age 3 or 4). If t represents the number of years since study entry, the formula for discounting a cost or benefit in year t to produce its present value is as follows:

$$\text{present value} = \frac{\text{value of benefits in year } t \text{ in real dollars}}{(1 + \text{discount rate})^{t-1}}$$

In this analysis, the calculation of present value was slightly more complicated than indicated by this formula, because the starting points were different for children entering at age 4 and children entering at age 3. Therefore benefits measured in the same year for these two groups of children were received 1 year later (counting from the time of program entry) by those beginning the program at age 3. Thus, present value of benefits for the group as a whole was calculated to represent the weighted average of present values for the 1-year and 2-year groups, (based on the numbers of children attending 1 and 2 years, respectively.)

From the formula, it should be clear that the calculation of present value reduces the value of benefits that came later relative to the value of costs that came earlier. For example, if the real discount rate is 5%, the present value of real-dollar benefits (or costs) in year 2 would be calculated by dividing those benefits (or costs) by $(1 + .05)^{2-1}$, or 1.05. The divisor would be 1.05 squared (1.1025) for calculating present value of year 3 benefits (or costs). For year 4, the divisor would be 1.05 cubed (1.1576). For year 15, it would be 1.05 to the 14th power (1.9799); for year 25, it would be 1.05 to the 24th power (3.2251). In other words, using a 5% real discount rate, the present value of a benefit received 15 years after the start of the program would be roughly one half of its real-dollar value, and the present value of a benefit received 25 years after the start of the program would be less than one third of its real-dollar value.

The correct real discount rate for the calculation of present value in the benefit-cost analysis of public programs is a matter of some debate among economists, and even the federal Office of Management and Budget and the U.S. General Accounting Office do not seem to agree (Kolb & Scheraga, 1990; Lind, 1982; Mikesell, 1977; U.S. General Accounting Office, 1992). Because the debate shows no sign of being resolved to the satisfaction of all parties, we conducted this analysis using real discount rates ranging from 0% to 11%. This encompasses the entire range of rates having serious advocates, and therefore one can make use of the analysis whatever one's view about the appropriate discount rate (Kolb & Scheraga, 1990). Remember that *real discount rates* are the rates *above* inflation, so if inflation is 4% per year, this 0% to 11% range corresponds to observed (nominal) interest rates of 4% to 15%. The author's view is that a strong case can be made for using a real discount rate of 3% and that real discount rates in the range of 3% to 7% are most reasonable (Gramlich, 1981; Kolb & Scheraga, 1990; Lind, 1982; U.S. General Accounting Office, 1992). Thus, this monograph first presents present values calculated with discount rates of 3%, 5%, and 7% throughout, and then, in the section on sensitivity analyses, it examines the effects of higher rates.

After the present value of each cost and benefit has been calculated, the present values of all of the costs and benefits can be aggregated to yield estimated net present value. If the benefits are greater than the cost, net present value is positive, and the High/Scope Perry Preschool program can be said to make a positive economic contribution to society as a whole. This does, in fact, turn out to be the case, and this finding holds for all real discount rates up to 11%. We can conclude from this result that the High/Scope Perry Preschool program was a sound public investment and compares favorably with many alternative uses of society's resources.

Describe the Distributional Consequences

Policies and programs differ in their distributional consequences — in who gains and who loses — as well as in their net effect on society as a whole. Although the net present value of a program can be the same regardless of whether it benefits everyone equally, benefits the poor more than the rich, or benefits the rich at the expense of the poor, people and their political representatives are not indifferent to these distributional differences. To make this cost-benefit analysis as useful as possible, the distribution of costs and benefits is described for two politically relevant groups — *study participants,* who were children from very low-income minority families, and the *general public,* who paid for the program as taxpayers.

This distributional breakdown was considered useful for two reasons. First, the goal of the program was to improve the educational, and thereby the long-term economic and social, success of children whose prognosis for educational and economic success was relatively poor. It is important to assess the preschool program's performance in achieving this goal. Second, the general public is not purely altruistic, and therefore it is important to investigate the extent to which indirect effects of the program contributed to the well-being of those who paid for the program. It is easier to persuade taxpayers and their representatives to support a program if it appeals to their self-interest as well as to their altruism.

Conduct Sensitivity Analyses

In every benefit-cost analysis, the analyst must make some assumptions in order to produce estimates of costs and benefits. At any given time, one or more assumptions might prove to be invalid, and changes in the assumptions might have substantive effects on the conclusions derived from the analysis. In some cases there might be theoretical or empirical disagreement about the validity of an assumption; in other cases an assumption might involve an uncertain prediction about the future. The role of sensitivity analysis is to identify critical assumptions and then explore what effects on study conclusions some reasonable variations in assumptions could have. The reason for doing so is twofold: (1) to reveal the extent to which the conclusions would stand if other assumptions were employed and (2) to indicate what conditions would have to hold in the future in order for the project to be a sound investment (sometimes steps can be taken when the project is implemented to ensure that such conditions hold).

Sensitivity analyses conducted for this benefit-cost analysis examined a wide range of alternative assumptions. Some analyses were specific (e.g., examining the impact on earnings estimates beyond age 27 of alternative assumptions about rates of productivity growth), while others were general (e.g., examining the impact of using alternative discount rates). Such analyses provide considerable information about the robustness of the conclusions with respect to variations in the assumptions. Because the results turn out to be highly robust, only the implications of extreme changes in assumptions that reduce benefit estimates are reported in the section on sensitivity analyses.

Although a specific section of Chapter 4 is devoted to sensitivity analysis, two key elements of sensitivity analysis come up throughout the discussion of benefit estimation. As noted earlier, we present all benefit estimates using a range of real discount rates, and we report separate estimates of benefits up to age 27 and benefits beyond age 27. Because the estimates beyond age 27 are projections and therefore less certain than those based on data up to age 27, reporting them separately allows the reader to judge the relative importance of the two sets of estimates for the analysis. In the extreme, it is possible to drop the beyond-age-27 benefit estimates altogether.

II Estimated Costs and Benefits: Program Costs, Child Care, and Education

This chapter provides an estimate of the High/Scope Perry Preschool program's cost and addresses the issue of how much a preschool program should cost today. In addition, it presents estimates of the benefits from the child care that was provided by the program and from the reductions in the overall cost of education. Benefits from child care were considered relatively unimportant when the study began in the early 1960s. Today the majority of families seek child care for their young children, and welfare reform proposals seek to move even more mothers of young children into the labor force. Therefore, child care benefits have the potential to be increasingly important.

Program Costs

The High/Scope Perry Preschool program has been described in a series of publications of the High/Scope Educational Research Foundation. The earliest publication, *Preschool Intervention* (Weikart, 1967), was followed by several monographs on the High/Scope Perry Preschool Project (Schweinhart et al., 1993; see also Berrueta-Clement et al., 1984; Schweinhart & Weikart, 1980; Weikart et al., 1978; Weikart et al., 1970). These documents are the primary sources of information that we used to construct a description of the program's operation and resources. There was also substantial historical information available on the program's personnel and other resources, including cost data collected by Carol Weber in 1975 from the Ypsilanti Public School District and summarized in yet another High/Scope monograph (Weber et al., 1978).

Cost Estimation

The publications of the High/Scope Foundation just cited, together with the personal recollections of some of the program's teachers and administrators, are the basis for the program description we used in estimating costs. Information about program costs was obtained from several sources, including Ypsilanti School District budgets, the Ypsilanti School District's accounting department records, and the program's administrator. As already mentioned, much of this information had been collected in 1975 by Carol Weber. These sources provide information about the program costs borne by taxpayers but not about any costs that may have been borne by the participants. Program records concerning the time parents spent in various program activities are the primary source of information about costs to program participants.

Table 4, which summarizes the results of the cost estimation, presents cost estimates for each year of the program, with a breakdown of costs by resource category and a calculation of cost per child. It should be noted that in each year but the last, there were two waves of study children in the program. In 1966–67 there was only one wave of High/Scope Perry Preschool study children, although there were 11 other children attending the program. Table 4 reports as program costs only those costs for the *study* children.

Table 4

COSTS OF THE HIGH/SCOPE PERRY PRESCHOOL PROGRAM
IN EACH YEAR'S CURRENT DOLLARS

Category	1962–63	1963–64	1964–65	1965–66	1966–67
Instructional staff	$25,853	$26,251	$27,764	$29,778	$16,832
Administrative and support staff	1,134	1,100	1,425	1,500	768
School district overhead	1,722	1,600	2,100	2,225	1,188
Classroom supplies	480	480	480	480	250
Developmental screening	234	115	120	120	0
Interest and depreciation on facilities	2,337	2,236	2,272	2,815	1,387
Total	$31,760	$31,782	$34,651	$36,918	$20,425
Number of children	21	20	25	25	12
Cost per child	**$1,512**	**$1,589**	**$1,386**	**$1,477**	**$1,702**
Cost per child in real 1992 dollars	**$7,611**	**$7,849**	**$6,692**	**$6,906**	**$7,596**

The cost estimates for the High/Scope Perry Preschool program are quite complete and include both operating and capital costs. Operating costs included those for *instructional staff, administrative and support staff, school district overhead, classroom supplies,* and *developmental screening.* Capital costs for the classrooms and other school district facilities were estimated in the form of imputed *interest and depreciation on facilities.* A detailed explanation of cost estimation is provided for each of these major cost categories.

Instructional staff costs are the costs of employing 4 teachers each year and include teacher salaries, fringe benefits, and the employer share of the Social Security tax. Because they were based on staff qualifications and seniority and on provisions of the school district contract with teachers, instructional staff costs varied from year to year. The actual salary figures for the preschool teachers were obtained from the Ypsilanti School District's accounting files, and the employer's share of the Social Security tax was calculated on the basis of these salary figures. At the time of the High/Scope Perry Preschool program (1962–1967), state contribution to a retirement plan was the only fringe benefit, and this was determined as a percentage of teacher salary. Therefore these percentages (obtained from the Michigan Public School Employees Retirement System) were also applied to the teacher salaries. Table 5 presents the calculation of instructional staff costs by year. Because only 12 of the 23 children in the 1966–67 preschool class were study participants, instructional staff costs were prorated for that year.

Administrative and support staff costs represent the contribution of nonteaching special education staff to the preschool program, including the management of the program by the Special Services Director. These costs were estimated in each year's current dollars by using the average per child cost of the Director's office for 1968–1969 and adjusting for inflation. The

Table 5

INSTRUCTIONAL STAFF COSTS (IN EACH YEAR'S CURRENT DOLLARS)

Category	1962–63	1963–64	1964–65	1965–66	1966–67
Teacher salaries (individual)	$6,260	$5,720	$6,270	$7,700	$7,720
	6,150	6,490	6,160	5,710	6,178
	6,040	6,270	6,930	6,930	8,260
	5,600	5,830	6,380	7,150	7,365
Total salaries	$24,050	$24,310	$25,740	$27,490	$29,523
State retirement fund payments					
State contribution as % of salaries	5.00%	5.12%	5.16%	5.79%	5.89%
Total state contribution (4 teachers)	$1,203	$1,245	$1,328	$1,592	$1,739
Employer-paid Social Security					
Maximum taxable earnings	$4,800	$4,800	$4,800	$4,800	$6,600
Total taxable earnings (4 teachers)	$19,200	$19,200	$19,200	$19,200	$25,978[a]
Employer tax rate	3.125%	3.625%	3.625%	3.625%	3.85%
Total Social Security (4 teachers)	$600	$696	$696	$696	$1,000
Total instructional staff costs					
Salaries	$24,050	$24,310	$25,740	$27,490	$29,523
Retirement fund	1,203	1,245	1,328	1,592	1,739
Social Security	600	696	696	696	1,000
Proportion of preschoolers in the study (if less than 100%)	—	—	—	—	12/23
Total	$25,853	$26,251	$27,764	$29,778	$32,262

[a]Includes one salary of $6,178, which is below the maximum taxable earnings level.

year 1968–69 was the earliest one for which the data needed to calculate per child cost were available. Data were obtained from Ypsilanti Public School District annual audit reports or budgets (Weber et al., 1978, p. 308). Table 6 on the next page presents the estimation of administration and support staff costs.

School district overhead costs account for the preschool program's share of general administrative and nonteaching staff, maintenance, utilities, and other general school system costs. Data for overhead were obtained from the Ypsilanti Public School District annual audit reports. An average overhead cost per child was calculated using the total numbers of children in the school system (Weber et al., 1978, p. 49), and this average cost figure was applied to the preschool program. The resulting estimation of total overhead costs for the preschool program is presented in Table 7.

Table 6

SPECIAL SERVICES ADMINISTRATIVE AND SUPPORT STAFF COSTS
(IN EACH YEAR'S CURRENT DOLLARS)

Year	Cost per Child[a]	Number of Students	Total Cost
1962–63	$54	21	$1,134
1963–64	55	20	1,100
1964–65	57	25	1,425
1965–66	60	25	1,500
1966–67	64	12	768

[a]Calculation of cost per child is based on the 1968–69 average of $72 per student, a total of $43,747 for 609 students. The special education budget includes a director, a secretary, and special education support staff.

Table 7

SCHOOL DISTRICT OVERHEAD COSTS (IN EACH YEAR'S CURRENT DOLLARS)

Year	Average Overhead Cost per Student	Number of Students	Total Overhead
1962–63	$82	21	$1,722
1963–64	80	20	1,600
1964–65	84	25	2,100
1965–66	89	25	2,225
1966–67	99	12	1,188

Classroom supplies is the category that accounts for the costs of equipping the classroom each year. This includes the costs of food for daily snacks as well as costs of materials used by the children. Since $480 was allotted annually to the preschool program for classroom supplies, this is the figure reported for each year in Table 4. Like instructional staff costs, supply costs were prorated for 1966–67.

Developmental screening costs account for testing and interviewing to select a sample that was economically disadvantaged and had a relatively poor prognosis for educational success. To select children for both the experimental and the control groups, 50 children were screened for each wave at a total cost of about $250. The costs of screening included in Table 4 have been prorated to reflect only that share of the $250 attributable to those who attended the preschool program. Calculations used to obtain the prorated costs are shown in Table 8.

Although the costs of screening are clearly part of the costs of performing the experiment, it is less clear that they should be considered to be part of the cost of program provision. If screening to select a disadvantaged sample was essential to securing the level of benefits observed in this experiment (i.e., if program benefits would have been lower for a sample of

Table 8

PROGRAM GROUP'S SHARE OF SCREENING COSTS
(IN EACH YEAR'S CURRENT DOLLARS)

Wave	Number in Program Group	Number in No-Program Group	Program Group as % of Total	Screening Costs Total for Both Groups	Total for Program Group	Per Program-Group Member
Zero	13	15	46%	$250	$116	$ 9
One	8	9	47	250	118	15
Two	12	14	46	250	115	10
Three	13	14	48	250	120	9
Four	12	13	48	250	120	10

children selected *without* screening — which is something we do not know), then screening costs are properly included as a program cost. If screening was not essential to the benefit level of the program group, even if screening had *some* direct effect on benefits — for example, by giving children in both groups experience in test-taking, screening costs would not properly be included. This is because the control group, whose benefits are compared with the experimental group's benefits, was also screened. We made the former, more conservative assumption; so screening costs for the experimental group are included as part of the cost of the program.

Capital costs consist of imputed **interest and depreciation** on fixed assets. Imputed **interest** is calculated to account for the income foregone when fixed assets were employed in the preschool program. In other words, we assumed that if these assets had not been used for the preschool program, they would have been used to benefit society in some other way. Therefore, these foregone benefits are considered to be costs of the preschool program and are accounted for by imputing interest on the fixed capital. For this analysis, we assumed an implicit interest rate of 3.5%. **Depreciation** is calculated to account for the decrease in value of the fixed capital due to wear, age, and other causes. Straight-line depreciation is used (e.g., 10% each year for 10 years). Because depreciation rates vary with the type of assets, we assumed a 10% rate for all equipment and a 3% rate for buildings, based on Internal Revenue Service asset guideline periods and other information on the useful life of school property (Schultz, 1971).

There are two categories of fixed capital to be considered for the preschool program. One is the equipment purchased for initial setup of the preschool classroom. The value of this equipment was $1,000 in 1962, and the combined implicit interest and depreciation rate for this classroom equipment was 13.5%. The other category of fixed capital is the Ypsilanti Public School District's physical plant and general equipment. We assumed that preschool students shared approximately equally with other students in use of this fixed capital. To figure depreciation for this second category, it was necessary to determine the distribution of school district assets by type. Table 9 shows this distribution for each year for which it could be ascertained. Based on the average distribution, a weighted average of 3.7% was

Table 9

DISTRIBUTION OF FIXED CAPITAL OF YPSILANTI PUBLIC SCHOOL DISTRICT

	% in Each Category		
Year	Land	Buildings	Equipment
1979–80	3.85%	83.86%	12.30%
1978–79	4.01	83.17	12.82
1977–78	3.67	83.06	11.27
1976–77	4.16	84.46	11.37
1975–76	6.25	80.39	13.36
1974–75	6.79	80.33	13.38
1973–74	5.90	81.53	12.57
Average percentage	4.95%	82.69%	12.44%
Depreciation rate	0.00%	3.00%	10.00%
Weighted average[a]	0.00%	2.48%	1.24%

[a]Weighted average equals the *average percentage* multiplied by the *depreciation rate*; the sum of the weighted averages across the three categories is 3.72%.

obtained for the depreciation rate, resulting in a rate of 7.2% for combined implicit interest and depreciation. The calculation of interest and depreciation for each year, using these rates, is presented in Table 10.

In addition to program costs borne by the public, a preschool program could involve costs to be borne by children and parents. Such costs were negligible for the High/Scope Perry Preschool program. There were no fees, school supplies were provided, and transportation was merely a matter of walking to the neighborhood school. The only resource sought from parents was time for the home visits, and participation in the visits was voluntary. Parents could (and did) choose not to receive a visitor or not to participate in a visit, in which case the teacher worked with the child alone. However, the visits did offer parents direct benefits in the form of positive social interactions with the teacher and information about parenting, education, and community services. On balance, participation is taken to imply that parents valued these immediate benefits (which are not included in the analysis) at least as much as the alternative activities they could have pursued in the 90 minutes required by each visit.

Thus, the figures in Table 4 (on p. 20) can be taken to represent all of the costs of the High/Scope Perry Preschool program. After the implicit price deflator for Gross Domestic Product for state and local government purchases (U.S. Bureau of Economic Analysis, 1993) was used to adjust Table 4 current-dollar cost estimates for inflation, we obtained these estimates in 1992 dollars: a cost per child of $7,601 for 1 year (Wave Zero only) and $14,415 for 2 years (averaging across Waves One to Four). Weighting the 1-year and 2-year cost estimates by the percentage of children in each wave yields a $12,888 average cost per child across the entire program group. Because benefit estimates are based on the program effects for all waves, the weighted-average cost estimate is the most appropriate figure for comparison with benefits. The present value of this weighted-average cost per child

Table 10

CALCULATION OF IMPLICIT INTEREST AND DEPRECIATION
(IN EACH YEAR'S CURRENT DOLLARS)

Category	1962–63	1963–64	1964–65	1965–66	1966–67
School district assets (thousands)	$10,386	$10,393	$10,489	$10,593	$10,982
Number of students[a]	7,132	7,132	7,205	7,146	7,264
Assets per student	$1,456	$1,457	$1,456	$1,482	$1,512
Number in program group	21	20	25	25	12
Program assets per year	$30,582	$29,145	$36,395	$37,056	$18,143
Implicit interest and depreciation					
On school district fixed capital[b]	$2,202	$2,098	$2,620	$2,668	$1,306
On classroom equipment[c]	$ 135	$ 138	$ 142	$ 147	$ 81
Total	$2,337	$2,236	$2,762	$2,815	$1,387

[a]Number of students for 1962–63 was not available, so 1963–64 number was used as an estimate. Numbers for 1965–66 and 1966–67 represent full-time equivalents.

[b]Program assets per year times 7.2%, the rate of implicit interest plus depreciation.

[c]Initial investment in classroom equipment was $1,000; combined rate of interest and depreciation was 13.5%, yielding $135 interest and depreciation in 1962–63 dollars.

is $12,356 at a 3% discount rate, $12,022 at a 5% discount rate, or $11,705 at a 7% discount rate.

The figures in Table 4 reveal that the number of children in the program, and thus the cost per child, varied from year to year. This was due to fluctuations in the number of 3-year-olds added to the program group each year as Waves Zero, One, Two, Three, and Four entered the study. The *number of children* shown for each year in Table 4 is what that year's cost estimate is based on, and it is the number of program participants who continued in the study beyond the preschool period. This is a conservative measure of class size for estimating cost per person for comparison with benefits per person. However, because a few children in the study were lost prior to completion of the preschool program, the actual number of children who attended the program each year was somewhat higher. Essentially, this analysis includes the costs of serving those children but assumes that *no benefits* were produced for them. Thus, the program's lowest cost-per-child figures in Table 4, which are based on a staff-child ratio of 1 teacher for 6.25 children (in 1964–65 and 1965–66), are the most appropriate to use in planning services. They provide the best basis for comparison with other programs.

Alternative Approaches and a Perspective on Cost

The weighted-average program cost estimate discussed here was designed to represent the actual cost of the program, based on the resources used and the prices paid for those resources. Actual salaries (current at the time) for the 4 teachers were converted to real 1992 dollars using the GDP implicit price deflator. An alternative approach would have been to estimate salary costs by using the national average salaries and benefits that were current at the time of estimation (1992) for the types of staff employed in the High/Scope Perry Preschool program. However, such an approach has the disadvantage that as updated benefit-cost analyses are produced, depending on the year of estimation, the estimated cost of the program could vary, because it would depend on whatever the national average teacher compensation was at the time of analysis.

Another issue that arises with respect to the most appropriate teacher compensation figure to use in the cost analysis is that teachers' salaries vary across school systems and across levels within a system. On the one hand, one could argue that because teachers in the High/Scope Perry Preschool program were experienced public school teachers, average public school teacher compensation (salaries plus benefits) should be used in the analysis. On the other hand, it might be even better to use average teacher compensation for preschool teachers in areas with high concentrations of disadvantaged children (i.e., areas like the one that the High/Scope Perry Preschool program was in), but estimates of the salaries and benefits of such teachers are not readily available. Alternatively, one could argue that most preschool teachers are paid much less than public school teachers and that teacher quality is only weakly related to this salary differential; therefore, for purposes of estimating preschool program costs to inform public policy, it would be appropriate to use the lower compensation rates of preschool teachers in general or, perhaps, the compensation rates of teachers in programs accredited by the National Association for the Education of Young Children (NAEYC).

The potential impact of using alternative current figures for teacher compensation can be investigated through fairly simple calculations. For example, assuming an average public school teacher salary of $34,945 (National Center for Education Statistics, 1993) and fringe benefits equal to 20% of salary (U.S. Bureau of Labor Statistics, 1992; Woodbury & Hamermesh, 1992), the estimated cost of the High/Scope Perry Preschool program would be roughly $9,000 per child per year, about 20% higher than the $7,601 one-year estimate used here. Assuming an average preschool teacher salary of $16,497 (the General Accounting Office's 1990 estimate for NAEYC-accredited centers, adjusted for inflation) and fringe benefits equal to 20% of salary, the estimated cost would be roughly $4,300 per child, about 40% lower than the one-year estimate of $7,601.

The key question with respect to program cost is this: What would it cost now to replicate the High/Scope Perry Preschool program? In answering this question, it must be recognized that today some additions to the program might be required. Because in many communities it is not possible for all children to walk to preschool, transportation would have to be added to the program. Also, to meet working parents' needs for full-time child care, the program would need to have longer hours of operation. Both of these factors would increase program costs. At the same time, if the program is to be feasible on a large scale, consideration must be given to modifications that would hold its cost down. This raises the question of how cost might be lowered without significantly reducing the program's effectiveness.

Clearly, cost can be lowered dramatically by such modifications as providing only 1 rather than 2 years of preschool education, foregoing the home visits, holding double sessions each day, increasing class size, using some lower-paid teacher assistants in lieu of teachers, using only one teacher in each classroom, and paying teachers less than public school salaries. Each of these structural changes, however, is a cause for concern. There is potential loss of program efficacy whenever there are changes in the nature and frequency of children's interactions with teachers, peers, and the physical environment (Bruner, 1980; Howes, Phillips, & Whitebook, 1992; Ruopp, Travers, Glantz, & Coelen, 1979). However, how such changes affect the benefits of a preschool program cannot be empirically identified with precision at this time.

In the absence of clear data regarding the impact of cost-cutting on children, government and other providers have employed all of the possible cost-reduction strategies anyway. It is difficult to argue against known cost-savings on the basis of hypothetical benefit-losses of unknown size. To keep costs down, preschool programs for disadvantaged children depart from the High/Scope Perry Preschool program model in almost all dimensions. Head Start, private preschool programs, and public and private child care programs pay considerably lower salaries and benefits to teachers. Most preschool programs have larger class sizes. Head Start and public school preschool programs provide most of their participants with only 1 year of service at age 4. Public school preschool programs pay salaries and benefits comparable to those paid in the High/Scope Perry Preschool program, but they have much larger class-sizes, and if they staff the classroom with more than one person, they use a teacher and an aide rather than two teachers. Public policy has strayed so far from the model that the risk of severely reduced benefits seems obvious. Further research on the effects of cost-saving measures on program effectiveness and benefits is needed.

Child Care

All early childhood programs, whether they are called preschool education or child care, simultaneously provide both education and custodial care (defined as having an adult attend to the health, safety, and comfort of the child in the absence of the parent). However, early childhood programs vary greatly in the amount and quality of education and custodial care they provide. The High/Scope Perry Preschool program was designed to provide high-quality education and only incidentally provided custodial care. With the benefit of hindsight, we can see that the inattention to such care was probably a mistake even in 1962, as evidenced by the 2 children who were unable to attend the preschool program because of their mothers' employment. Nevertheless, the program provided a certain amount of custodial child care free of charge, which allowed parents to concentrate on other activities while their child was in attendance.

The market value of child care provided by the High/Scope Perry Preschool program was estimated based on survey data for hourly child care payments from several years later (Rodes, 1975; Rodes & Moore, 1975). Updated to real 1992 dollars, the estimated market value is roughly $1.50

per hour, or $435 per child per year, allowing for absences. The present value of the weighted-average benefit is $738 per child at a 3% discount rate, $722 at a 5% discount rate, or $702 at a 7% discount rate. This estimated child care benefit is quite small. However, it should be recognized that at the time the High/Scope Perry Preschool program was launched, child care — particularly full-day child care — was rare, as was full-time employment outside the home for mothers of young children (Low & Spindler, 1968; U.S. Bureau of the Census, 1982).

Today, child care is much more common, and most mothers of young children are employed outside the home, many of them full-time. Thus, the potential custodial child care benefits of preschool programs are an important consideration and should be considered in the design of programs. Welfare reform emphasizing training and work will further increase the need to take into account families' child care needs and the value of child care benefits when developing programs to serve disadvantaged children like those in the High/Scope Perry Preschool program. A program providing full-day, year-round child care would produce annual child care benefits of $3,750 per child in real 1992 dollars, based on the same $1.50 per hour figure applied earlier. This amount is substantial enough to offset much if not all of the cost of expanding a high-quality preschool program from part-day to full-day.

Elementary and Secondary Education

A complete discussion of the data and methods used to estimate the effects of the High/Scope Perry preschool program on the costs of elementary and secondary education is presented here. Because no new data on elementary and secondary education were obtained after the age-19 benefit-cost analysis (Barnett, 1985b), the estimation of the preschool program's effects on the costs of elementary and secondary education is essentially unchanged from the previous analysis. However, there are several minor ways in which the final estimates have been updated to differ from those used at age 19. After a review of the basic data and procedures, these differences are explained.

Overview

To estimate the effects of the High/Scope Perry Preschool program on the costs of elementary and secondary education, we constructed individual educational histories for 112 study participants for whom official school records could be obtained. These histories provide a year-by-year record of the school attended, grade level, type of educational program or track, extent and type of special education services, diagnostic testing and other special-education-related services, and disciplinary incidents. Cost data for each type of educational service in each year were then mapped onto the educational histories to produce year-by-year cost histories for each individual participant.

Except for the few cases in which students were placed in special residential schools or other institutions, the school costs that we mapped onto individual education histories were from the Ypsilanti Public School District. Costs of the relatively rare "outplacements" were estimated on the basis of the amounts that sending schools were charged for those placements. The Ypsilanti district accounted for 80% of the years of schooling of study participants. Most of the remaining years of study participants' schooling were in three other surrounding districts (Ann Arbor, Willow Run, and Van Buren), but it was not possible to obtain *detailed* cost data for all years (1963 to 1980) from these other districts. In fact, detailed cost data from the Ypsilanti schools were available only because such data (for students' earlier years) had been collected in 1975 by Carol Weber for the first benefit-cost analysis of the High/Scope Perry Preschool program (Weber et al., 1978). Had it been possible, using the actual detailed cost data from the three other districts would not have had much impact on our overall cost estimate, because costs in surrounding districts were not very different from those in Ypsilanti.

As with the preschool program cost estimates, an alternative approach would have been to use national-average cost data to estimate the program's effects on elementary and secondary education costs. However, it would have been difficult to obtain national averages specifically for districts with high percentages of disadvantaged students, rather than simple national averages; and even the best available simple national averages would have been almost a decade old (Moore, Strang, Schwartz, & Braddock, 1988). An additional complication is introduced by the fact that since the time when study children were in school, the percentage of children placed in special education has risen, and costs of special education placements have risen relative to costs of regular education placements. Exactly how this alters the expected effects of preschool programs on education costs for disadvantaged children is difficult to determine. For example, we do not know exactly how changes in special education, such as those that have come about since the years of the High/Scope Perry Preschool program, would have affected the assignment of the study children to various types of compensatory and special education programs. But it seems likely that if anything, the increased costs and other changes in special education over the years have *increased* the benefits to be obtained from preschool education's effects on elementary and secondary schooling costs.

It is noteworthy that because the High/Scope Perry Preschool program's estimated effect on schooling costs is based on individual cost histories, it reflects relatively fine-grained differences in school experiences that are not captured by the analyses of school outcome measures conducted by Schweinhart et al. (1993). Their outcome analyses examined the number of years of special education, the number of special education classifications by type of disability, the grade retention rates, and the dropout rates. In contrast, this cost analysis takes into account differences in cost among seven types of educational placements: regular classroom, regular classroom plus speech-and-language services, regular classroom plus compensatory education, special education classroom, integrated special education, alternative (disciplinary) school, and special schools. The cost analysis also takes into account effects of the *timing* of educational placements. For example, costs of special education placements and grade retentions are higher the earlier they occur, because early occurrence of costs means that their present value is higher. Thus, even if preschool program attendance only *delayed* a child's grade retention or special education placement, it would result in some cost savings after discounting.

Cost estimates were produced for each school year from 1963–64 to 1979–80 for each of the following program categories:

1. **General education** — the "normal" educational program in a regular classroom, with no extra educational services on a regular basis

2. **Special-classroom special education** — often referred to as "self-contained" special education, a program where more than 50% of the child's time in school is spent in a special classroom for those with educational handicaps

3. **Integrated special education** — involving a "teacher-consultant," "helping teacher," or "crisis teacher," a program where more than 50% of the child's time in school is spent in a regular classroom

4. **Speech-and-language support** — in addition to the regular classroom, regular therapy for speech and language difficulties

5. **Compensatory education** — in addition to a regular classroom, remedial reading and/or math instruction

6. **Disciplinary education** — placement in an alternative public school setting as a result of delinquent behavior

7. **Special school** — placement outside the regular school system to provide more-intensive services on either a daytime or a residential basis

Because these categories were formulated to capture differences in cost among educational programs, they do not correspond exactly to categories that would be drawn based on type of educational handicap or other educational difficulty. There is, however, some correspondence. Children who are classified as educably mentally impaired (EMI), emotionally impaired (EI), or learning disabled (LD) may be assigned to either a *special-classroom special education* program or an *integrated special education* program. *Speech-and-language support* and *compensatory education* deal with less severe impairments and are, at face value, more impairment-specific. The *disciplinary education* category is quite problem-specific, although the characteristics of the actual programs provided to these students have varied. Finally, *special school* placement appears to be most frequently associated with the most severe behavioral problems.

Using these cost categories captures most of the cost differences between regular and special education programs. However, it does not capture the cost of the additional psychological testing received by students under consideration for special education placement. Therefore a cost for psychological testing was added to the cost of a study participant's school year whenever the school record indicated such testing or whenever a participant who was not in a special classroom, integrated special education, or a special school program was assigned to such a program the following year. Some other cost differences may remain uncounted because there is no way to estimate them from the available data. Probably the most important uncounted cost differences are due to the extra teacher time that "problem children" receive in regular classrooms or the toll that such children take on other children in the classroom. Indeed, the magnitude of such costs is one reason some children are completely removed from the regular classroom.

Calculation Procedure

A single general procedure (involving a set of assumptions) was used to calculate costs for the seven program categories for each year from 1963–64 to 1979–80. This general procedure comprised the following steps:

1. School district costs were separated into operating costs and capital costs.

2. Operating costs were separated into instructional and noninstructional costs.

3. Noninstructional costs were divided by the number of full-time equivalent (FTE) students, yielding a figure for noninstructional cost per student.

4. Implicit interest and depreciation were calculated for school district fixed assets, and their total was divided by the number of FTE students, yielding a figure for capital cost per student.

5. Noninstructional cost per student and capital cost per student were added to yield a figure called overhead per student.

6. Instructional costs were allocated to each of the public school cost categories (costs for special school are calculated separately) as indicated by the school district's budget and staffing (e.g., four teachers for special classrooms, five for integrated classrooms). Instructional cost for each category was divided by number of FTE students to yield instructional cost per student.

7. The additional cost of administration and support services (except for psychological testing) was allocated to students who received special-classroom special education, integrated special education, and speech-and-language support. Total special education administration and support service cost was divided by total special education FTEs to yield the special education overhead per student.

8. **General education** cost per student was calculated as the sum of overhead per student and general education instructional cost per student.

9. **Special-classroom special education** cost per student was calculated as the sum of overhead per student, special education overhead per student, and special-class instructional cost per student for early years, when all instructional time was in a special class. For later years, when some instructional time was spent in regular class, a weighted average of full-time equivalent special-class cost and regular-class cost was calculated.

10. **Integrated special education** cost was calculated first on a full-time equivalent basis as the sum of overhead, special education overhead, and integrated special education instructional costs. A weighted average of full-time equivalent integrated and general education costs was calculated on the basis of the percentage of time spent in regular class.

11. **Speech-and-language support** cost was calculated in the same way as integrated special education cost, using the appropriate instructional cost figure.

12. **Compensatory education** cost per FTE student was calculated as the sum of overhead and compensatory education instructional costs per FTE student. The cost per child for those in the compensatory education category was calculated as the weighted average of FTE compensatory and general education costs, based on the percentage of time spent in regular class.

13. **Disciplinary education** cost per FTE student was calculated as the sum of overhead and disciplinary education instructional costs per student. Again, for years when this program was not full-time, a weighted average with general education cost was calculated.

14. **Special school** costs were calculated on an individual basis for each school and year, based on specific cost estimates. In most cases, because there were established rates that these schools charged the state, actual cost figures were readily available.

In addition to the above cost categories, a cost was calculated for psychological evaluations. This was done, instead of simply including school psychologists in special education overhead, because a significant amount of the psychologist's time was spent evaluating students who were not placed in special education programs. We estimated the cost of a psychological evaluation by dividing the psychologist's annual salary/benefits total by 135, the estimated number of evaluations performed per year.

Not all the data needed for the procedure of estimating costs for each program category were available for every year. As might be expected, the earlier the year, the scarcer the appropriate data. Using the procedure just described, we were able to calculate general education costs (no special services) for every year, based on official data for each year. For most years, we were able to calculate costs for the other public school program categories based on official data, supplemented by personal recollections of school personnel, regarding the student-teacher ratios (or relative amount of instruction per student) in each program category. This procedure was used to calculate costs for special-classroom special education and compensatory education from 1969–70 to 1979–80, for integrated special education and speech-and-language support from 1970–71 to 1979–80, and for disciplinary education from 1969–70 to 1976–77. Table 11 presents all of those costs.

School district budget data for the remaining years were not detailed enough to permit cost calculation from individual program data. For these years, therefore, we based our cost estimates on regression equations relating general education costs to other program category costs in the years of

Table 11

EDUCATION COSTS PER CHILD-YEAR BY PROGRAM CATEGORY
(IN CONSTANT 1981 DOLLARS)

Year	General Classroom	Special-Classroom Special Education	Integrated Special Education	Speech-&-Language Support	Compensatory Education	Disciplinary Education
1979–80	$3,378	$4,670	$4,575	$3,734	$3,776	—
1978–79	3,075	4,101	4,163	3,395	3,504	—
1977–78	3,144	4,147	4,111	3,559	3,525	—
1976–77	2,914	4,365	3,907	3,658	3,264	$4,341
1975–76	2,824	4,073	4,075	3,231	2,999	3,687
1974–75	2,856	3,816	4,506	3,240	2,920	4,323
1973–74	2,779	3,608	4,247	3,080	2,846	3,559
1972–73	2,464	3,120	3,670	2,795	2,539	3,273
1971–72	2,155	3,264	4,267	2,564	2,256	2,932
1970–71	2,025	2,919	2,994	2,379	2,068	2,143
1969–70	2,196	3,359	—	—	2,279	2,900
1968–69	2,263	—	—	—	—	—
1967–68	2,101	—	—	—	—	—
1966–67	1,920	—	—	—	—	—
1965–66	1,853	—	—	—	—	—
1964–65	1,711	—	—	—	—	—
1963–64	1,653	—	—	—	—	—

Note. Source is Barnett (1985b).

more-complete data. Table 12 on the next page presents the full set of costs, including those estimated from the data in Table 11. Because special program placement tended to occur in the later years of schooling, the cost figures estimated by regression analysis entered into the benefit-cost analysis less frequently than did those calculated directly from official data. This was especially true of the disciplinary program, where the estimates for the early and also the most-recent years (when such programs fell into disfavor) were rarely used.

Using the costs for each program category by year, we were able to estimate each year's education cost for each participant by mapping the appropriate costs onto the individual educational histories described on page 28. As stated previously, special school costs were estimated on a case-by-case basis. When a student's educational history indicated participation in more than one program category simultaneously (e.g., special classroom for EMI and a teacher-consultant for EI), we calculated the costs for that child by adding the original cost (above the cost of a regular classroom) of each additional placement to the full cost of the primary placement. Based on the assumption that children with multiple special services receive the same amount of each special service as do children with a single placement, this

Table 12

EDUCATION COSTS PER CHILD-YEAR, INCLUDING ESTIMATED YEARS
(IN CONSTANT 1981 DOLLARS)

Year	General Classroom	Special-Classroom Special Education	Integrated Special Education	Speech-&-Language Support	Compensatory Education	Disciplinary Education
1979-80	$3,378	$4,670	$4,575	$3,734	$3,776	$4,574
1978-79	3,075	4,101	4,163	3,395	3,504	4,164
1977-78	3,144	4,147	4,111	3,559	3,525	4,257
1976-77	2,914	4,365	3,907	3,658	3,264	4,341
1975-76	2,824	4,073	4,075	3,231	2,999	3,687
1974-75	2,856	3,816	4,506	3,240	2,920	4,323
1973-74	2,779	3,608	4,247	3,080	2,846	3,559
1972-73	2,464	3,120	3,670	2,795	2,539	3,273
1971-72	2,155	3,264	4,267	2,564	2,256	2,932
1970-71	2,025	2,919	2,994	2,379	2,068	2,143
1969-70	2,196	3,359	3,654	2,581	2,279	2,900
1968-69	2,263	3,247	3,701	2,650	2,439	3,065
1967-68	2,101	3,058	3,587	2,482	2,264	2,845
1966-67	1,920	2,847	3,460	2,296	2,069	2,600
1965-66	1,853	2,769	3,412	2,227	1,997	2,509
1964-65	1,711	2,604	3,312	2,080	1,844	2,317
1963-64	1,653	2,536	3,272	2,021	1,781	2,239

Note. Source is Barnett (1985b).

produced an exact accounting of cost. In a few cases, the assignment of costs was complicated because records did not clearly indicate whether the student received special-classroom or integrated special education. In these cases, we assigned the mean cost for the two categories.

The effect of the High/Scope Perry Preschool program on elementary and secondary education costs was estimated from the 112 individual educational cost estimates by the method of ordinary least squares (OLS). Cumulative cost is the dependent variable, and preschool program attendance (yes/no) is the independent variable.

Separate estimates of the effect on schooling costs were produced for males and females. Table 13 presents these estimates, first undiscounted and then discounted at real rates of 3%, 5%, and 7%. These figures are essentially the same as those reported in the economic analysis at age 19 (Barnett, 1985b, Tables 17 and 18). The new estimates for males and females have simply been adjusted for inflation (updated from 1981 to 1992 dollars), and the discounted figures were weighted to produce present-value estimates for the sample as a whole instead of separate present-value estimates for 1- and 2-year samples. To adjust for inflation, we used the GDP implicit price deflator for state and local government purchases. Another, more important change from the age-19 analysis is this: Previously, the final estimate for the effect of

Table 13

ESTIMATED EFFECTS OF THE HIGH/SCOPE PERRY PRESCHOOL PROGRAM ON ELEMENTARY AND SECONDARY EDUCATION COST PER CHILD (IN REAL 1992 DOLLARS)

Discount Rate	Cost-Saving Effect on Males	Cost-Saving Effect on Females	Cost-Saving Average Effect
1992 dollars discounted at 0%	$13,520	$5,898	$9,709
1992 dollars discounted at 3%	9,461	4,282	6,872
1992 dollars discounted at 5%	7,512	3,638	5,575
1992 dollars discounted at 7%	5,998	2,884	4,441

the preschool program was a weighted average based on the proportions of males and females in the sample (Barnett, 1985b). For the present analysis, the final estimate is the simple average of the two numbers — the estimated effect for males and the estimated effect for females. The *average effect* column of Table 13 shows this simple average.

The *average effect* estimates in Table 13 are somewhat smaller than those that would have been produced using the weighted-average method followed in the age-19 analysis. This difference arises because the estimated effects were larger for males than for females, and males were a larger portion of the study sample. Thus the *simple average* is larger than the weighted average obtained from equally weighting the effects for each gender. For comparison, in the age-19 benefit-cost analysis, the undiscounted estimate of the effect adjusted to 1992 dollars is a cost reduction of $10,923 per child, whereas the undiscounted estimate based on the current method is a cost reduction of $9,709 per child. One reason that estimated cost savings for elementary and secondary education are lower for females than for males is that, compared with no-program females, program females were much less likely to drop out before high school graduation. This greater persistence of program females in the last years of high school partially offset the cost savings that were due to their decreased need for special services and other factors. Program males were no different from no-program males with respect to high school completion.

Adult Secondary and Higher Education

Adult Secondary Education

Adult secondary education is a category of educational cost and benefit that was not included in earlier benefit-cost analyses because of a lack of information. By age 27, however, some study participants who had not completed high school by age 19 had enrolled in adult education courses, including adult high school and GED preparation classes offered by high schools. Thus we were able to obtain data on adult secondary education from their school records. The cost of adult secondary education was estimated based on the number of courses study participants had taken (though credit need not have been received) and an estimated cost of $1,710 (in 1992 dollars) per adult education class. Although it might have been possible to estimate the cost of adult education from data on the specific adult education programs at schools actually attended, the additional precision this might have provided for the estimation of a very small benefit was not deemed to justify the additional effort that it would have required. It was difficult to obtain any data at all on the costs of adult education; the $1,710 per course estimate was based on a $623 estimate of instructional cost per adult-education class in the 1978–79 school year (Varden, 1982). To obtain an estimate of total cost, we increased this instructional cost figure by 20% (a reasonable figure for overhead). The resulting estimate of total cost was then converted to 1992 dollars.

The program group had a lower rate of participation in adult secondary education than did the no-program group. The High/Scope Perry Preschool program is estimated to have reduced the cost of adult education by an undiscounted $532 per person ($275 for males, $789 for females). The present value of this estimated per person reduction in adult education cost is $283 at a 3% discount rate, $188 at a 5% discount rate, or $127 at a 7% discount rate. Because the estimated benefit from reduced adult education costs is a tiny fraction of all estimated benefits, error in the estimate for the cost of adult education could have only a trivial effect on the overall results of the benefit-cost analysis.

Higher Education

Although effects on higher education costs were estimated in the economic analysis at age 19, there was little evidence to use in the analysis at that time. Thus, the age-19 analysis was based on entry to higher education at age 19 and on projections from national data regarding the extent to which college entrants continued their education. This method was far from satisfactory, but it was all that could be done with the available data. By the time of the age-27 study, we could reasonably assume that study participants had completed virtually all of their higher education. Therefore, in this analysis, costs of higher education for program and no-program groups were estimated based entirely on attendance data up to the age-27 data collection. We made no projections of higher education costs beyond age 27, because these were judged likely to be minimal. Any participants entering higher education after age 27 would have only a small impact on costs. At the time of the age-27 interview, only 2 people in the sample had taken a course recently enough that one might argue that they were continuing higher education (participation of some others was quite sporadic). With no clear trends in the data indicating otherwise, we proceeded on the simple assumption that there would be no further higher education.

The primary sources of information about higher education attendance were the official transcripts of 30 of the 39 persons who had reported receiving higher education. For persons for whom transcripts were not obtained (the college either did not respond or failed to find the required transcript), we estimated the number of credits of course work based on data for students whose transcripts *had* been obtained. This was necessary because participants tended to report the number of years in which they had any higher education attendance, and this was not always a good measure of their full-time-equivalent (FTE) higher education. Much of their attendance was part-time. Consequently, the years of FTE higher education for those without transcripts (and without a degree) were estimated by prorating the number of years they reported. The factor used for prorating was the ratio of *actual credits enrolled* to *reported years of higher education* for those with transcripts.

To produce an estimate of the higher education cost for each individual, we combined data on the individual's number of courses, credits, and type of institution attended with estimates of the average costs per FTE student for public 2-year colleges and 4-year colleges. Virtually all of the higher education obtained by study participants was in public institutions. Given the large differences in costs between 2-year and 4-year institutions, it was essential to distinguish between them in cost estimation. However, we made no distinction between the costs of 2-year non-credit college courses that may have been taken in preparation for obtaining a GED and other 2-year college courses. Sources of cost data for 2- and 4-year public institutions were the National Center for Education Statistics (1992, 1993) and Cohn and Geske (1990). Table 14 presents the cost estimates (per FTE student) applied to higher education in each year from 1976 to 1992.

The estimated effects of the High/Scope Perry Preschool program on higher education costs were considerably different for males and females. For females, the preschool program was estimated to *increase* the cost of

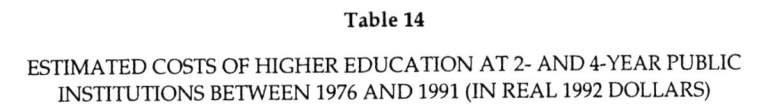

Table 14

ESTIMATED COSTS OF HIGHER EDUCATION AT 2- AND 4-YEAR PUBLIC INSTITUTIONS BETWEEN 1976 AND 1991 (IN REAL 1992 DOLLARS)

Year	2-Year	4-Year
1976–77	$6,380	$12,281
1977–78	6,423	12,386
1978–79	6,524	12,548
1979–80	6,449	12,691
1980–81	6,089	12,313
1981–82	6,056	12,190
1982–83	5,750	11,905
1983–84	5,789	11,949
1984–85	6,257	12,488
1985–86	6,367	12,745
1986–87	6,397	12,620
1987–88	6,250	12,701
1988–89	6,338	12,689
1989–90	6,338	12,689
1990–91	—	12,689
1991–92	—	12,689

Table 15

ESTIMATED EFFECTS OF THE HIGH/SCOPE PERRY PRESCHOOL PROGRAM ON
HIGHER EDUCATION COST PER PERSON (IN REAL 1992 DOLLARS)

Discount Rate	Cost-Saving Effect on Males	Cost-Saving Effect on Females	Cost-Saving Average Effect
1992 dollars discounted at 0%	$747	−$3,896	−$1,575
1992 dollars discounted at 3%	492	−2,227	−868
1992 dollars discounted at 5%	375	−1,555	−590
1992 dollars discounted at 7%	287	−994	−354

Note. Because *increases* in costs are negative "cost savings," the estimated effects for females and for the group as a whole are expressed as negative numbers.

higher education by an undiscounted $3,896 per person. For males, the preschool program was estimated to *decrease* the cost of higher education by $747 per person. These results reflect male-female differences in both number of classes attended (measured in terms of semester credits) and distribution of classes between 2-year and 4-year institutions. The estimated average effect across both genders is a per person cost increase of $1,575 (undiscounted). Table 15 presents these figures as well as the present values of the estimated effects, based on discount rates of 3%, 5%, and 7%. Because *increases* in costs are negative "cost savings," the Table 15 estimated effects for females and for the group as a whole are expressed by negative numbers.

Two of the assumptions made in estimating higher education costs tended to produce a slightly larger estimate of the amount by which the High/Scope Perry Preschool program increased higher education costs. First, if we had assumed there would be further higher education for the two persons reporting fairly recent higher education experience at age 27, this would have increased costs for the no-program group. Second, if instead of relying on self-report when official transcripts could not be obtained, we had estimated the program's effect based only on those with official transcripts, the estimated increase in higher education costs due to the preschool program would have been smaller. However, neither alternative would have had a substantial impact on the results, given the small size of higher education effects relative to other costs and benefits.

III Estimated Costs and Benefits: Employment, Crime, and Welfare Assistance

Employment, crime, and welfare assistance are among the central concerns of American society today, and they each have enormous economic implications. The High/Scope Perry Preschool program had long-term effects in each of these domains. This chapter addresses the economic implications of these effects.

Employment and Earnings

Data from the age-19 and age-27 surveys provided evidence that the High/Scope Perry Preschool program led to long-term improvements in the economic circumstances of males and females who had attended the program. Taking into account program versus no-program differences that were statistically significant at the .10 level in a two-tailed test (equivalent to .05 in a directional one-tailed test of significance), the study found that at age 19, program participants were more likely to have a job, had higher earnings (largely because they were more likely to have a job), were more likely to consider themselves self-supporting, and were more likely to report having some savings. At age 27, program participants had higher earnings, were more likely to own a second car, and were more likely to be homeowners. The finding of greater earnings held for both males and females despite the females' much higher marriage rates (a factor that one might expect to reduce labor force participation).

The primary focus of this part of the analysis is the preschool program's contribution to increased compensation from employment in the form of earnings and fringe benefits. Direct evidence is available only on earnings. Self-report data on earnings were obtained from the age-19 and age-27 interviews. At age 19, study participants described their jobs and reported hours of work, pay rate, and months of employment for their four most recent jobs. Because respondents began reporting with their current job and worked backward, this reporting procedure tended to underestimate earnings prior to age 16 (Barnett, 1985b). However, the extent of underreporting was judged to be quite small, and the impact on the estimated effect of the preschool program was minimal. In a few cases, age-19 survey data were supplemented with additional data on wages. For example, military pay-scales were used to provide salary data for those reporting their rank in the military, and clarifications of apparent contradictions were obtained by follow-up calls to some study participants (Barnett, 1985b, p. 60). The data collected at age 19 were used to estimate earnings for age 16 through age 19.

Earnings Through Age 27

The same kinds of employment and earnings data were collected from respondents at age 27 as at age 19. Study participants were asked about job history — hours of work, pay rate, and months of employment for their current employment and for any other jobs they could remember having over the previous 5 years. In addition, respondents were asked to report their total income from employment for the "past month" and for the "past 12 months." As would be expected, respondents' recall was better for their more recent jobs, and the number of subjects who reported earnings and employment data for more than 3 years at the age-27 interview was too small to provide reasonable estimates for the groups prior to age 25. Moreover, those who recalled 4 years or more of earnings and employment data tended to be atypical (for example, people who held the same job the entire period or who never had a job). Thus, the self-reported job history data from the age-27 interview were used to estimate earnings for ages 25 through 27 but not for ages 20 through 24. Even for ages 25 through 27, the earnings data were not always complete and were clarified with data on education, welfare, and imprisonment when such supplementation seemed reasonable (e.g., when no wage was reported, but the employment was clearly a minimum-wage job; or when job data were not provided, but the respondent was in prison at the time).

Table 16 reports estimated earnings by group and gender for ages 16 through 19 and ages 25 through 27 (adjusted to 1992 dollars using the GDP implicit price deflator). These figures indicate that participation in the High/Scope Perry Preschool program increased earnings but produced much larger increases for females than for males. This result is consistent with the estimated effects on educational attainment and predicted by a substantial body of economic research on the relationship between education and earnings (e.g., Cohn & Geske, 1990; Hill, 1981; Mincer, 1974). As noted earlier, the preschool program produced a large increase in educational attainment for females, but no effect on educational attainment was found for males. Because education level is a key determinant of employment and earnings, it makes sense that the female program participants showed a much greater increase in earnings.

Overall, for females in the study, the education histories, the self-reported earnings and employment data at the time of interview, and the earnings and employment histories were internally consistent and easily explained. From the age-27 interview data, it appears that program females earned more than no-program females primarily because the former were more likely to be employed. Possibly there was some small additional contribution from a tendency to earn more money if they *were* employed, which could have been due to earning a higher rate of pay or working more hours. These earnings outcomes are exactly what one would expect, based on the superior educational outcomes of the program group. Also, the earnings effect estimate that is based on the detailed employment data is remarkably close to the earnings effect estimate that is based on reported monthly earnings at the time of the interview.

For males, the results were somewhat more complicated and difficult to interpret. Program males obtained about the same number of years of education as did no-program males, so little or no difference in their earnings would be expected on this account. Thus, it is mildly surprising to find that the preschool program had an effect on male earnings between ages 19 and 27, although the estimated effect was relatively small and somewhat irregular. A possible explanation for this difference in earnings is that even though they did not stay in school any longer than no-program males, dur-

Table 16

ESTIMATED MEAN ANNUAL EARNINGS AT AGES 16 THROUGH 19 AND AGES 25 THROUGH 27 BY GROUP AND GENDER (IN REAL 1992 DOLLARS)

Age	Program Females	No-Program Females	Program Males	No-Program Males
16	$ 190	$ 705	$ 95	$ 302
17	1,203	723	1,039	1,116
18	1,944	833	3,410	3,953
19	6,174	2,909	9,480	8,944
25	12,372	8,387	17,669	13,165
26	13,614	9,607	13,621	13,987
27	14,308	8,620	16,397	16,064

ing their time in school the program males obtained a better education and acquired greater abilities. Evidence for such a preschool program effect on the quality of education can be found in the program males' higher achievement test scores. Other studies have found quality-of-education differences to have adult-male-earnings effects independent of years of education (e.g., Kuh & Wadsworth, 1991).

An additional complication is presented by the preschool program effect on male earnings that we estimated based on an analysis of the "past month's" earnings reported in the age-27 interview. This estimated effect — an increase of $538 per month — when extrapolated to an entire year amounts to increased annual earnings of $6,456, which is much greater than the $1,490 annual effect we estimated from the job history data. Because there is no significant difference in program and no-program males' reported employment rates at age 27, the preschool program's positive effect on monthly earnings would appear to be entirely due to higher rates of pay, longer hours worked, or more-regular employment for those with jobs.

It is difficult to know what to make of the differences between the two estimates of program effect on male earnings. On the one hand, the job history questions probed for details that respondents might otherwise not have recalled, and the questions did not require them to make mental calculations to estimate their total annual earnings — both factors that should have increased the accuracy of their reports. On the other hand, respondents whose employment had been somewhat irregular might have forgotten relevant details over time, and the resulting errors in their reporting might have affected the estimated differences between the groups. As noted earlier, the information provided in response to the job history questions was incomplete, and our efforts to fill in missing data with estimates may have been less successful for males than for females.

Males' job history earnings estimate and "past month's" earnings estimate can be compared with an estimate based on a third source of earnings data — the question asking respondents to report total income for the past year. Responses to the "past 12 months" question produced an estimate of program effects on earnings that was closer to the estimate obtained from the job history data. However, this similarity could mean merely that it was no easier for respondents to accurately recall the past year's total earnings than for them to accurately recall work schedules and wage rates for the past several years.

To conduct another check on the earnings estimates for males, we compared the sample-based estimates with estimates provided by data on earnings reported by 25- to 29-year-old Black[1] males in the Current Population Survey (CPS, U.S. Bureau of the Census, 1992a). Estimates based on CPS earnings figures and educational attainment were roughly consistent with the estimates based on the sample members' job history data. This correspondence with national survey data provides another source of confidence in the job history data. However, collection of the CPS data required of respondents the same kind of extended recall and construction of a total earnings estimate as the age-27 survey's "past 12 months" earnings question, so CPS data might be thought to suffer from the same kind of reporting problems.

Ultimately, there is no conclusive evidence that can be brought to bear to determine which male earnings estimate is the most accurate. For this analysis we chose to estimate earnings through age 27 for both males and females based on the detailed job history data. This offered the advantage of consistency, provided the most data (covering 3 years), and seemed to be the most conservative approach because it produced a smaller estimated effect on earnings than we would have obtained by using "past month's" earnings reported at age 27. In other words, we chose to risk underestimating, rather than overestimating, the preschool program's effect on earnings.

The annual earnings figures in Table 16 were only part of what we needed for a complete estimation of the High/Scope Perry Preschool program's effects on earnings and employment. To estimate earnings effects over an entire lifetime, we also required estimates for earnings between ages 19 and 25 as well as beyond age 27. We estimated the former (earnings for ages 20 through 24) by assuming a linear trend in real earnings between ages 19 and 26 for each of the four groups defined by program attendance and gender (program females, no-program females, program males, and no-program males). We used age 26, rather than age 25, as the upper endpoint of this interval because average earnings across ages 25, 26, and 27 (for which earnings figures were available) provided a more reliable estimate than did the age-25 figures alone, given the high degree of variability across the three ages. This procedure produced earnings figures that yielded the following estimates for the undiscounted effects of the preschool program on earnings through age 27: $38,713 per female and $8,887 per male. Therefore, the estimated average preschool program effect on earnings through age 27 was an increase of $23,800 per person (undiscounted).

---

[1] The author uses the term "Black" occasionally because it was used by the Census Bureau in collecting and summarizing the data.

Earnings Beyond Age 27

For the years beyond age 27, it was necessary to project earnings based on educational attainment. For two reasons, we projected earnings only through age 65: (1) The small numbers of persons employed after age 65 make it difficult to obtain reliable earnings estimates for African-Americans by gender and education, even for a broad category such as ages 65 to 74 (U.S. Bureau of the Census, 1992a). (2) The importance of any effects on earnings beyond age 65 was minimal because discounting greatly reduces the value of earnings beyond age 65 (discounting at 3% yields present value that is only about 15% of the undiscounted amount at age 65); furthermore, the relatively few people employed beyond age 65 results in only a tiny fraction of lifetime income being earned after age 65.

Three types of data were combined to project earnings beyond age 27: (1) data relating African-Americans' educational attainment to their mean annual earnings by age and gender in 1991, (2) data on African-Americans' survival rates (percentages of specific birth cohorts projected to remain alive at various ages) by age and gender, and (3) the High/Scope Perry Preschool study's estimates of the educational attainment of program and no-program males and females at age 27. Data relating educational attainment to 1991 earnings by age and gender were obtained from the March 1992 CPS (U.S. Bureau of the Census, 1992a). Survival rates were obtained from a report by the National Center for Health Statistics (1993).

The procedure used to project earnings beyond age 27 is the standard approach to estimating lifetime earnings from educational attainment (Miller & Hornseth, 1967). First, from the March 1992 CPS, we obtained estimates of earnings by age (for ages 28 through 65), gender, and 6 categories of educational attainment (9–11 years of schooling, 12 years of schooling, some college but no degree, 2-year degree, 4-year degree, and graduate study). Then, these earnings estimates were weighted by the percentage of persons in the sample, with each level of educational attainment in the four groups defined by program attendance and gender. Finally, the weighted earnings estimates for each age by group were adjusted based on the probability of survival to each age. This produced an estimate of earnings per person for each of the four groups for each year from age 28 to age 65.

We applied the same survival rates to program as to no-program study participants alive at age 27, even though a small difference in survival rates between the program and no-program groups had already been introduced by the pre-age-27 deaths of 2 no-program females. Because the participants who died contributed no earnings beyond age 27, they were included in the following way in the number of no-program participants used to calculate earnings per person: Their earnings were estimated as zero dollars for ages 28 through 65, and this lack of earnings was incorporated into the estimation of the preschool program's effect on earnings beyond age 27. It is difficult to judge whether the two groups' observed difference in survival by age 27 was in any way related to participation in the preschool program; in any case, because it involves only 2 participants, our decision about how to handle the difference in survival has very minor consequences for the results. The program group would be predicted to have a higher survival rate because by age 27 it was better-educated and involved in less delinquency and crime, but *how much* these two differences from the no-program group will affect survival rates beyond age 27 is impossible to predict with any precision. Our use of the same survival rates for both groups probably tends to underestimate the preschool program's effect on earnings.

Using a growth rate to adjust the cross-sectional earnings figures upward as age increases is part of the standard procedure for projecting lifetime earnings from cross-sectional data on earnings and education. This growth-rate adjustment anticipates any future increases in worker productivity that would lead to wage growth. In the benefit-cost analysis at age 19, we used real annual growth rates of 0%, 2%, and 3.5% to explore the effects of adjusting for productivity growth. We judged the 2% rate to yield the best estimates of projected lifetime earnings because, at the time, a 2% real rate approximated the real growth in national income per person over most of the period since World War II (Barnett, 1985b).

In more recent years (1980 to 1992) the performance of the economy and the growth of real earnings per person has been distinctly lower than 2%. Although there is considerable uncertainty about the extent to which this earnings stagnation signals a long-term decline in the rate of economic growth, and although some of the stagnation in real earnings growth may have been due to the rapid rise in the cost of fringe benefits, for the benefit-cost analysis based on the age-27 study, we judged it prudent to make no adjustment for real growth in projecting earnings beyond age 27 (Levy & Murnane, 1992). Thus, this analysis makes the conservative assumption that there will no growth in real earnings over the next 40 years. This implies, for example, that improvements in the quality of education across generations will have no effect on productivity and earnings.

Our earnings projections are conservative for another reason: They make no adjustments for changes in women's labor force participation (rate of employment and hours worked). However, women's employment rates and working hours have been increasing for some time. Despite stagnation in wage rates, this has produced gains in their *annual* earnings (Levy & Murnane, 1992). Although the rate of increase of women's labor force participation appears to be slowing, it is by no means played out and can be expected to produce further increases in women's annual earnings over the next several decades. Thus, the assumption of no growth in projected annual earnings is particularly conservative for women and seems likely to lead to underestimation of the effects of the preschool program on the earnings of females beyond age 27. Evidence that projecting women's earnings from cross-sectional data has indeed produced sizeable underestimates for previous decades has been provided by the U.S. Bureau of the Census (1983).

Based on the assumptions just described, the projected earnings beyond age 27 for study males and females are those shown in Table 17. (The most reasonable alternative assumptions about productivity and women's labor force participation would have increased these projected earnings estimates substantially, as shown in Chapter 4 under "Sensitivity Analyses.") Comparing the estimates of projected earnings of program and no-program males reveals a small negative effect (decreased earnings) for program males. Although this effect is small compared with the program's positive effect on females' projected earnings, it is inconsistent with the positive effect on male earnings up to age 27. This inconsistency is the result of our projecting male earnings based on educational attainment alone, because a small, statistically insignificant difference in educational attainment favored no-program

Table 17

PROJECTED LIFETIME EARNINGS BEYOND AGE 27
(IN REAL 1992 DOLLARS)

Discount Rate	Program Females	No-Program Females	Program Males	No-Program Males
1992 dollars discounted at 0%	$509,000	$418,000	$621,000	$636,000
1992 dollars discounted at 3%	144,000	117,000	172,000	176,000
1992 dollars discounted at 5%	66,000	54,000	79,000	81,000
1992 dollars discounted at 7%	32,000	26,000	38,000	38,000

Note. Earnings are discounted to age 4 only. Each estimate can be discounted to age 3 by dividing by $1 + r$, where r is the relevant discount rate.

males. Because theory and past empirical research provide no reason to think that this small educational attainment difference was due to the program as opposed to random fluctuation, and because the projected negative earnings effect was strongly contradicted by the estimated effect on earnings based on self-report in the age-27 interview, we decided against using the projections for males presented in Table 17.

This left two alternatives for projecting male earnings beyond age 27. One was to use the sample data for earlier years to project male earnings for future years. The other was to assume that there was no effect on male earnings beyond age 27. Table 18 presents the estimated average effects on earnings beyond age 27 (for males and females) based on these two alternative assumptions for males. Given the limitations of the earnings data for males through age 27, the most defensible course was to assume no effect on male earnings beyond age 27. Even if further analysis had revealed the intervening variables linking the preschool program with increased earnings for males, national data linking any variables other than educational attainment to earnings by age, gender, and ethnicity would not have been available to us. Producing a better estimate of the preschool program's effect on lifetime earnings remains an important task of future research on the High/Scope Perry Preschool study sample.

Table 18

ESTIMATED PROJECTED (AGE 28–65) PROGRAM EFFECTS ON PER PERSON
EARNINGS OF PROGRAM PARTICIPANTS (IN REAL 1992 DOLLARS)

Discount Rate	Earnings Increase Assuming Negative Effect on Male Earnings	Earnings Increase Assuming No Effect on Male Earnings
1992 dollars discounted at 0%	$38,000	$45,500
1992 dollars discounted at 3%	11,240	13,194
1992 dollars discounted at 5%	4,815	5,778
1992 dollars discounted at 7%	2,848	2,848

Other Employment-Related Benefits and Total Compensation

As noted earlier, increased earnings are not the only benefits associated with improvements in earnings. Research on the relationship between education and job characteristics indicates that the effects of increased educational attainment also include higher fringe benefits and greater nonpecuniary occupational benefits, such as higher occupational status, greater job satisfaction, better working conditions, and greater convenience (Duncan, 1976; Mathios, 1988). The only one of these benefits that could be estimated and valuated for this analysis was fringe benefits, or more precisely, costs paid by the employer over and above salary. Costs paid by the employer for the employment of the worker include both traditional fringe benefits and government-imposed costs, such as the employer's share of the Social Security tax.

Although the High/Scope Perry Preschool study's interviews provided no direct measures of fringe benefits and other employer costs, the effects of the preschool program on these benefits can be estimated from national data relating these additional costs to wages and salaries (U.S. Bureau of Labor Statistics, 1992; Woodbury & Hamermesh, 1992). Since 1980, traditional fringe benefits have averaged 18% or more of salary across all jobs (Woodbury & Hamermesh, 1992). Other major costs paid by the employer include Social Security tax, worker's compensation, and unemployment insurance; these equal roughly 12% of salary. Thus, total compensation equals nearly 130% of salary (U.S. Bureau of Labor Statistics, 1992). The Social Security tax alone added from 6.13% (in 1980) to 7.65% (in 1989) to total compensation.

Of course, fringe benefits tend to be lower for low-paying jobs, and the High/Scope Perry Preschool study participants for the most part had relatively low-paying jobs. Data on the lowest paying service jobs in 1992 (an average of $6.30 per hour) indicated that their fringe benefits were equal to only about 9% of wages and that other employer-paid costs brought total nonwage benefits to almost 24% of wages (U.S. Bureau of Labor Statistics, 1992). Based on these data, the High/Scope Perry Preschool program's effect on total compensation (earnings plus fringe benefits and other employer-paid costs) was estimated to equal 120% of the effect on salary.

This approach to estimating the value of total compensation is considered conservative but advisable because of the relative uncertainty involved in estimating fringe benefits and other costs. The total compensation estimate is conservative in three respects. First, the 20% figure we used is low relative to estimates of the fringe benefits and other employer-paid costs of even low-paid workers. Second, although the percentage of total compensation accounted for by fringe benefits increases as earnings rise, the method we used to estimate the effect on total compensation assumes that it is strictly proportional to the effect on wages. Third, we made no adjustment for the value to the employee of nonpecuniary benefits from employment (Duncan, 1976; Mathios, 1988).

Table 19

PROGRAM EFFECTS ON PER PERSON LIFETIME EARNINGS AND
TOTAL COMPENSATION (IN REAL 1992 DOLLARS)

Discount Rate	Increase in Earnings Through Age 27	Increase in Earnings Age 28–65	Increase in Lifetime Earnings	Increase in Lifetime Compensation[a]
1992 dollars discounted at 0%	$23,800	$45,500	$69,300	$83,160
1992 dollars discounted at 3%	12,082	13,194	25,276	30,331
1992 dollars discounted at 5%	7,795	5,778	13,573	16,288
1992 dollars discounted at 7%	5,082	2,848	7,930	9,516

[a]Earnings plus benefits that are estimated to be 20% of earnings.

Summary of Employment-Related Effects

Table 19 reports the estimated effects of the preschool program on earnings and total compensation discounted at various real rates. Estimates are presented for earnings through age 27, beyond age 27, and over a lifetime, as well as for total lifetime compensation. The estimated effects are sizeable even after discounting. On the whole, the procedures used to estimate the effects of the preschool program on employment-related benefits tend toward underestimation. Therefore, the figures in Table 19 can be considered lower-bound estimates of the present value of the program's effects.

The program group's advantages with respect to savings, auto ownership, and home ownership (mentioned at the beginning of this chapter) may not be entirely accounted for by the estimated increases in earnings. These other economic advantages could be due in part to differences in attitudes about economic responsibility or in ability to manage money and household finances. No direct measures of these attitude and ability variables are available. Also, it is reasonable to suppose that insofar as increased savings, auto ownership, and home ownership result from the program group's long-term improvements in employment and earnings, it is not only because of increased ability to save and spend but also because of improved access to credit. This would represent a real economic advantage for the program group, but it is difficult to estimate the dollar value of these benefits from the information available, which does not include data about study participants' total assets and liabilities, including homeowner equity.

Crime and Delinquency

Crime has become one of the most salient concerns of Americans in recent years. Only unemployment and economic stagnation rival crime in importance as political issues; and crime, like unemployment and economic stagnation, is an especially serious problem for the nation's most disadvantaged citizens. Economic measures of the impacts of crime provide one indication of the magnitude of the problem. Taking into account personal costs to victims, criminal justice system costs, and costs of private security measures, the estimated annual cost of household and personal crime in the United States exceeds $200 billion (Cohen, 1988; Zedlewski 1987). The direct costs of crime to business (and, thereby, consumers) and some of the other costs of household and personal crime are not included in this figure. The overall cost of crime to society is undoubtedly much greater than $200 billion per year.

Data from self-report and official records provide evidence that the High/Scope Perry Preschool program significantly reduced crime and delinquency over time (Schweinhart et al., 1993). These data make it is possible to estimate the economic benefits of the preschool program's effects on crime. The benefits from a reduction in crime and delinquency include

1. Reduced victim costs because fewer people suffer the direct effects of crime and delinquency
2. Reduced costs of criminal justice system efforts to prevent crime, apprehend criminals, adjudicate those apprehended, and imprison and otherwise monitor those convicted
3. Reduced costs of private security and similar measures (guards, locks, alarms, insurance) taken to avoid crime
4. Reduced feelings of fear and insecurity; increased ability to enjoy private or public spaces that one might avoid for fear of victimization

Unfortunately, the dollar value of some of these benefits could not be estimated. National data on crime and its costs enabled us to estimate the impact of the preschool program on only the first two of these four types of crime costs. Our analysis had to omit the program's effects on the latter two types of costs, which make up a significant portion of the costs of crime. It is unclear how private security costs and the psychological costs of fear, insecurity, and restricted enjoyment of the environment respond to changes in crime rates. Based on national figures from the sources just cited (Cohen, 1988; Zedlewski, 1987), this analysis, in its omission of private security costs alone, might underestimate the value of the preschool program's effect on crime by as much as 25%.

Benefits Through Age 28 From Crime Reduction

Like employment-related benefits, the crime reduction benefits were estimated in two stages — crime reduction though age 28 and crime reduction after age 28. Because the study collected crime data somewhat later than employment data, crime reduction data are available through age 28 rather than age 27. To estimate the High/Scope Perry Preschool program's effects on crime costs, we used criminal justice system records collected at ages 19 and 28. These records, which provide information about arrests, convictions, imprisonment, probation, and parole for the study participants, enabled us to construct individual crime and criminal justice system histories for the study participants through age 28 and to project crime patterns and costs beyond age 28. For both periods (through age 28 and after age 28), victim and criminal justice system costs were estimated separately.

For several reasons, study participants' arrests rather than their convictions were used to estimate crime costs. The most important reason was the availability of national data linking number of arrests to number of crimes actually committed, by type of crime. For example, victim surveys indicate that for every assault arrest, there are 5 assaults actually committed. These data allowed us to estimate the number of crimes committed by study participants based on the number of their arrests by type of crime. There are no available data linking number of crimes committed to *convictions* by type of crime, however. The program and no-program groups differ from each other in both number of arrests and number of convictions, but their difference in convictions is somewhat smaller. Although it is possible that committing fewer crimes is not the only reason that the program group has a lower arrest rate than the no-program group, no clear case can be made that their conviction rate would be a better indicator of their rate of crime commission. The frequent use of plea bargaining for reasons unrelated to guilt or innocence is only one factor that makes differences between arrests and convictions difficult to interpret.

Victim costs. As stated earlier, two categories of crime costs — victim and criminal justice system — were estimated separately for years up through age 28. Based on individual arrest data, we constructed crime histories listing number of crimes by type for each year for each study participant. Participants' self-report data from the interview were insufficient for this purpose, not only because of possible underreporting but also because of lack of data on *when* crimes were committed, which is critical for discounting. Individual data were then consolidated to produce arrest histories by age for four groups: program males, no-program males, program females, and no-program females. As mentioned in the previous paragraph, we estimated the number of crimes committed by each of the four groups at each age by combining individual arrest histories with national estimates of the number of victimizations for each arrest by type of crime. These national estimates were determined from 1990 data from two annual reports: *Criminal Victimization in the United States* (U.S. Bureau of Justice Statistics, 1992), which reports number of victimizations, and *Crime in the United States* (Federal Bureau of Investigation, 1992b), which reports number of arrests. The national estimates of victimizations per arrest (4 for rape, 5 for assault, 5 for arson, 10 for auto theft, 12 for robbery, 12 for larceny, and 14 for burglary) were applied to each participant's arrest history to produce estimates of total crime committed by type of crime at each age for the four groups. Applying the victim cost estimates for each type of crime to these histories produced crime cost histories. We then divided totals for the four groups by the number of persons in each group to produce estimates of victim costs of crime committed per person at each age through age 28.

Victim costs were estimated for rape, assault, bank robbery, robbery, burglary, auto theft, and larceny, but not for narcotics and other "victimless" crimes. Table 20 presents the victim cost estimates used in this analysis. They were obtained from Cohen (1988, 1990) and adjusted for inflation, to 1992 dollars. Because of the relative importance of crime costs, particularly victim costs, in the analysis, a summary of the derivation of Cohen's esti-

Table 20

VICTIM COSTS BY TYPE OF CRIME (IN REAL 1992 DOLLARS)

Type of Crime	Cost
Rape	$65,229
Arson	42,860
Bank robbery	24,031
Robbery	16,089
Assault	15,596
Auto theft	3,995
Burglary	1,191
Larceny	226

Note. Cost estimates from Cohen (1988) were adjusted for inflation to 1992 dollars. Estimates of the costs of personal and household larcenies were averaged to produce a single estimate.

mates is provided here. Cohen himself provides more-detailed explanations of the construction of his estimates and a thorough defense of his procedures.

Table 21 presents Cohen's original estimates (in 1985 dollars) and displays the breakdown of victim costs into three categories: *direct losses, pain and suffering,* and *risk of death.* The value of *direct losses* includes the value of property losses due to damage or theft, costs of medical services and psychological counseling, and costs of time lost from work; these are based primarily on data from the National Victimization Survey and information on the cost of injuries obtained from trial data. The value of *pain and suffering* was estimated from jury award data for specific physical and mental injuries (whether or not associated with crime) and data on the incidence of these injuries by type of crime. The value of the *risk of death* was based on the number of murders associated with each type of crime and the value of a life (estimated to be $2,000,000, based on studies of wage differentials associated with increased risk of death.)

Although better estimates of the costs of crime may be produced in the future, Cohen's estimates seem reasonable and were thus judged to be adequate for the task at hand. Cohen's use of jury award data in the estimation procedure seems likely to raise the most questions, because the media frequently report about people receiving what seem to be excessive jury awards. It should be borne in mind, however, that because the media are most likely to report only "newsworthy" (exceptionally high) awards, the public tends to obtain extremely biased information on this subject. Nevertheless, an important aspect of Cohen's approach is that he excluded punitive damage awards from the amounts used to estimate victim costs. According to Cohen (1990), punitive damage awards are the largest part of jury awards and the source of much controversy. To facilitate judgments about the reasonableness of the victim cost estimates, Table 21 sets out the components of the estimates. One indication of the likely direction of bias from Cohen's use of jury data is provided by the $600,000 average award for wrongful death of an adult. This is less than one third of the estimate that Cohen obtained for the value of a life using wage and employment fatality

Table 21

ESTIMATED VICTIM COSTS BY COMPONENT (IN REAL 1985 DOLLARS)

Crime	Direct Losses	Pain and Suffering	Risk of Death	Total Cost
Rape	$ 4,617	$43,561	$ 2,880	$51,058
Arson	14,776	6,393	12,380	33,549
Bank robbery	4,422	10,688	3,700	18,810
Robbery	1,114	7,459	4,021	12,594
Assault	422	4,921	6,685	12,028
Auto theft	3,069	0	58	3,127
Burglary	939	317	116	1,372
Larceny	176	0	1	177

Note. From Cohen (1988). Larceny estimates are averages for personal and household larcenies.

data. Of course, the impact of any problems with the *pain and suffering* and *risk of death* cost-estimates is limited by the relative infrequency of crimes such as arson, assault, and robbery — the ones likely to cause pain and suffering, or death. Many crimes have no estimated victim cost at all.

Because Cohen distributes costs of murder across all crimes (based on the relative frequency of the crime's association with murder, or the *risk of death*), it would have been inappropriate to estimate the cost of homicides separately, based on a value for loss of life. Instead, for purposes of victim cost estimation, the few homicides for which study participants were arrested were treated as assaults (the associated crime). This procedure, while it prevented double counting of both death and risk of death, also increased the stability of the analysis by allocating the cost of a crime for which people are rarely charged (murder) across the much larger number of crimes with which it is associated.

Finally, parts of the costs of crime can be thought of as "transfer payments" from victims to offenders and therefore as costs to crime victims but not to society as a whole. (Transfer payments are shifts of money or property from one person to another.) In this analysis, however, *all* of the costs to victims are treated as costs to society, for the following reasons: First, the transfers are forced and not voluntary, even from a societal perspective, and in societal impact they are not equivalent to other transfer payments, such as gifts or welfare payments. Second, it would be extremely difficult to determine what parts of the costs of crime might be considered to be forced transfers (such as theft), and these parts would in any case be a very small fraction of victim costs. For example, the value of stolen property is a relatively small portion of the costs of crime to victims, and the value that is transferred is much smaller than the value lost to the original owner due to loss of legal title. In addition to victim costs, some part of the criminal justice system's costs for incarceration (the prisoner's food, clothing, shelter) might be considered to be transfer payments. However, the value of these to the recipient not only is difficult to measure but also is surely reduced by the conditions under which these transfers are provided. No doubt most

Table 22

ESTIMATED CRIMINAL JUSTICE SYSTEM COSTS (EXCLUDING CORRECTIONS) BY TYPE OF CRIME (IN REAL 1992 DOLLARS)

Crime	Criminal Justice System (CJS) Cost
Murder	$57,739
Rape	30,730
Robbery	28,142
Burglary	13,586
Assault	6,308
Larceny	6,065
Auto theft	6,065
Narcotics	6,001
Other personal	1,747
Miscellaneous	2,135

Note. For lack of better information, the CJS costs of bank robbery and arson were estimated by the cost of robbery, and the CJS cost of rape was estimated as the average of costs for murder, robbery, and assault.

prisoners would be willing to exchange them for their freedom, and the value of lost freedom has not been included in the analysis.

Criminal justice system costs. We estimated criminal justice system costs through age 28 based on study participants' actual arrest, conviction, and incarceration histories. Police, prosecutorial, and court costs were estimated by combining individual arrest histories with data on costs per arrest for each type of crime. The estimates of criminal justice system costs per arrest (minus costs of corrections) were based on estimates obtained from Barnett (1985b) updated to 1992 dollars. Table 22 presents these estimates. Note that no criminal justice system costs were estimated for status offenses and traffic violations.

We were able to estimate the costs of corrections (incarceration and supervision of probation) by using records of study participants' time in prison or jail and on probation to first construct individual corrections histories by age. Corrections costs by age could then be estimated by applying to these corrections histories the estimates of costs of imprisonment and costs of supervision while on probation. The latter types of cost estimates we obtained from national data on costs of prison and probation supervision and numbers of persons in prison and on probation (U.S. Bureau of the Census, 1992b; Zedlewski, 1987). Estimates we used to estimate corrections costs were $20,000 (in 1992 dollars) per year of imprisonment for adults, $29,600 (in 1989 dollars) per year of imprisonment for juveniles, $600 (in 1990 dollars) per year of supervision associated with probation, and various other cost figures for juveniles (e.g., the cost of temporary detention) used in the previous benefit-cost analysis (Barnett, 1985b).

Crime Costs Beyond Age 28

To estimate the effects of the preschool program over a lifetime, it was necessary to project crime and its costs beyond age 28. The *Uniform Crime Reports* (Federal Bureau of Investigation, 1980, 1991, 1992a) provide cross-sectional data on arrests by age and sex. We used these figures to estimate the percentage of arrests occurring at each age through age 65. (Crimes and arrests decline with age so their numbers are negligible beyond age 65). Because the post-age-28 pattern of the percentage of arrests by age is nearly identical for men and women, we used the same estimates for both.

Because roughly 60% of all arrests occur by age 28, we considered costs through age 28 as representing 60% of the lifetime crime costs (undiscounted); the remaining 40% were projected through age 65 based on the percentage figures for arrest by age. The procedure we used to project costs was as follows: Total cost of crime per person through age 28 for each group by gender was divided by 0.60 (60%) to produce an estimate of total lifetime crime costs for each group. This figure was then multiplied by the percentage of arrests occurring at each age from 29 to 65 to produce an estimate of the cost of crime at each age by group and gender. For example, the estimated percentage of total lifetime crime costs attributed to age 29 was 3.5%, whereas it was 0.7% for age 45, and 0.1% for age 65.

This projection of crime costs has several limitations. One limitation is based on the fact that arrest rates change over time because of policy changes. Another is based on the fact that criminal behavior, including patterns over a lifetime, may change across cohorts. Both types of changes could result in differences between the projections based on cross-sectional data and what actually happens. In two respects, our projection procedures may underestimate the benefits of the preschool program. First, we projected that crime costs beyond age 28 would be strictly proportional to crime through age 28 for both groups by gender. However, it seems possible that compared with those having recent involvement in crime, those having no recent involvement in crime would be likely to produce fewer crime costs in the future. Thus, the approach we used would seem to overestimate the future crime costs of any program females who had one arrest at a young age and no other arrests through age 28. Second, because patterns of arrest by age were sufficiently similar across types of crime, we could use the pattern for all index crimes to project crime costs beyond age 28. However, national data on arrests indicate that the proportion of violent crimes committed beyond age 28 is somewhat greater than that for all crimes. Because violent crimes have higher costs, this might mean that we underestimate the preschool program's reduction of crime costs.

Summary of Crime Reduction Benefits

Table 23 presents estimated crime costs per person for males and females by preschool program participation. As can be seen, most of the costs of crime are estimated to have occurred by age 28, and victim costs account for most of the costs of crime to society. Except for the costs per program female, the estimated per person costs of crime are quite large. No-program

Table 23

ESTIMATED PER PERSON CRIME COSTS BY PROGRAM ATTENDANCE
AND GENDER (IN REAL 1992 DOLLARS)

Source of Cost	Victim Cost	Criminal Justice System Cost	Total Cost
Through age 28			
Program males	$ 56,505	$41,334	$ 97,839
No-program males	154,724	57,724	212,193
Program females	3,227	1,043	4,270
No-program females	50,987	17,385	68,372
Beyond age 28			
Program males	37,670	27,556	65,226
No-program males	102,979	38,483	141,462
Program females	2,151	695	2,846
No-program females	33,992	11,590	45,582

Table 24

PRESCHOOL PROGRAM'S ESTIMATED PER PERSON CRIME COST REDUCTIONS
(IN REAL 1992 DOLLARS)

Source of Cost Reduction	Victim Cost Reduction	Criminal Justice System Cost Reduction	Total Cost Reduction
Through age 28			
Males	$ 97,964	$16,390	$114,354
Females	47,760	16,342	64,102
Average	72,862	16,366	89,228
Beyond age 28			
Males	65,309	10,927	76,236
Females	31,841	10,895	42,736
Average	48,575	10,911	59,486
Lifetime			
Males	163,273	27,317	190,590
Females	79,601	27,237	106,838
Average	121,437	27,277	148,714

Table 25

PRESENT VALUE OF ESTIMATED PER PERSON CRIME COST REDUCTIONS
(IN REAL 1992 DOLLARS)

Source of Cost Reduction	1992 Dollars Discounted at:			
	0%	3%	5%	7%
Victimization				
Through age 28	$ 72,862	$40,161	$27,977	$19,097
Beyond age 28	48,575	17,423	9,154	4,945
Lifetime	121,437	57,584	37,131	24,042
Criminal justice system				
Through age 28	16,366	8,882	6,021	4,143
Beyond age 28	10,911	3,914	2,057	1,106
Lifetime	27,277	12,796	8,078	5,249
Total				
Through age 28	89,228	49,044	33,998	23,240
Beyond age 28	59,486	21,337	11,211	6,051
Lifetime	148,714	70,381	45,209	29,293

Note: Because of rounding, components may not sum to totals.

males were estimated to produce considerably more total crime costs than program males, though there is a relatively small difference between the two groups of males on criminal justice system costs. This is because the difference in arrests between the two groups of males appeared to produce little difference in incarceration, though it did produce a significant difference in post-release supervision costs. No-program females produced much larger crime costs than did program females. Although no-program females were much less involved in crime than their male counterparts, they did have more crime involvement than the program females, who had almost *no* involvement in crime. So the preschool program appears to have resulted in a sizeable reduction in crime costs for both women and men.

Table 24 presents the estimated effects of the preschool program on crime costs. Sizeable benefits from reductions in crime were estimated both before and after age 28, though more than half the benefits were obtained by age 28. Reductions in costs to victims accounted for approximately 80% of the preschool program's undiscounted benefits with respect to crime. One reason for this is that victim costs account for most of the costs of crime to society. Another reason may be that the amount of incarceration was not proportionate to arrests and crime. This would be consistent with the criminal justice system's difficulties accommodating the prison population. It is also consistent with the public perception that variations in sentencing are at best weakly related to criminal histories or to the danger that specific criminals pose to society.

Table 25 above shows the present value of each estimated crime cost reduction calculated at various discount rates. As would be expected, discounting substantially reduces the importance of projected cost reductions (i.e., cost reductions beyond age 28). Of course, when discounted at 3%, 5%, or 7%, the present value of the total lifetime cost reduction is considerably smaller than the undiscounted amount, because crime and delinquency first become serious problems when the participants are in their late teens and twenties, 15 to 20 years after their preschool years. Nevertheless, the present value of the estimated benefits remains large relative to the costs of program, and the crime reduction benefits would by themselves justify the preschool program on the basis of its economic return.

Welfare

Analyses of self-report and official records data collected at ages 19 and 27 indicate that the High/Scope Perry Preschool program affected participation in welfare (public assistance) programs. The major welfare programs from which study participants could have received benefits were Aid to Families with Dependent Children (AFDC), food stamps, Medicaid, and General Assistance (GA). The first three of these were federal programs providing cash (AFDC) or in-kind (food stamps and Medicaid) assistance to people with low incomes. The AFDC program was primarily available to single mothers and their children. Medicaid eligibility was largely linked to qualification for other benefit programs, and virtually all families receiving AFDC received Medicaid benefits. Food stamps were more broadly available. Although these were federal programs, states administered them, and federal and state governments shared the costs of the programs. The GA program, a State of Michigan program providing cash payments to low-income individuals without dependents, was eliminated sometime after the completion of the age-27 data collection.

Welfare Costs Through Age 27

To estimate the preschool program's effects on welfare costs through age 27, individual payment histories were constructed for AFDC, GA, and food stamps. The first step in developing these histories was to pool two kinds of data: (1) study participants' self-report data on welfare program participation and the amounts of welfare received and (2) official records on the amounts of AFDC, food stamps, and General Assistance received by study participants. These two data sources produced histories in which the amounts received and the dates of program participation were available for some years but not others. As explained below, additional data had to be used to construct more-complete histories.

Even for persons with active social services records at age 27, official records provided data on only a limited number of years. Study participants' self-report data on welfare payments provided the amounts received from the various welfare programs only at the time of the interviews. The most complete source of information on program participation was the self-reported "number of months of welfare assistance in the past 10 years," which covered the respondents' entire adult life to that point. We used study participants' data on employment, earnings, incarceration, and children's birth dates, together with eligibility rules, to identify the months each type of welfare assistance was received whenever this could not be determined from official records. Payment schedules for AFDC, food stamps, and GA, which were obtained from the State of Michigan, were used to estimate the amounts of monthly payments for each person receiving welfare.

All AFDC and some GA recipients automatically qualified for Medicaid or a state-operated ambulatory medical program. According to national data, virtually all AFDC recipients receive Medicaid services (Committee on Ways and Means, 1991). This was confirmed for this sample by self-report data and official records when available. Because Medicaid and similar state program payments are made directly to service providers, individuals — program beneficiaries — have no way of knowing what the costs are for the services they receive. However, state data were available on the average annual cost of these medical programs in 1991 for persons receiving AFDC and GA. We used these data to estimate the costs of medical programs for study participants for each month in which they received welfare assistance.

For 10 study participants, data on type, amount, and timing of welfare assistance were not available, but it was known that they had received welfare at some time. All except one were men, who would have been eligible for GA and food stamps but not AFDC. If the one woman among those 10 participants had received AFDC, this would have been found in the records, as it was for all of the other women reporting AFDC program participation. Therefore, we assumed that all 10 of the study participants had received GA and food stamps. We based estimates of the amounts received by these 10 participants on Michigan payment schedules and the average duration of welfare benefits for each group (program and no-program) by gender. When the date at which welfare was first received could not be determined from schooling, employment, or incarceration data, we assumed that the welfare assistance occurred at the earliest point at which the person could have qualified, because the probability of welfare program participation declines with age.

Welfare Cost Reductions Beyond Age 27

To estimate the preschool program's effect on welfare program participation over an entire lifetime, it was necessary to make projections beyond age 27. This was made difficult by the lack of data on very long-term program participation and uncertainty regarding the determinants of length of program participation (Duncan, Hill, & Hoffman, 1988; Ellwood, 1986; Gottschalk, 1992). Because Michigan eliminated its GA program shortly after the age-27 follow-up, we projected payments for AFDC, food stamps and Medicaid only.

The best data available for use in constructing projections about AFDC program participation come from the Panel Study on Income Dynamics (Ellwood, 1986). However, even these data cover only a 10-year period. By age 28, the High/Scope Perry Preschool study sample had already been potential welfare recipients for 10 years, and some had received welfare for the entire 10 years. Based on age patterns of welfare use found by Ellwood (1986) and Duncan (1988), we projected that persons receiving AFDC at the time of the age-27 interview (most of whom had been on AFDC for 8 or more years) had a 15% probability of exiting AFDC each subsequent year until age 50, when all AFDC participation was assumed to end. This projection produced a fairly rapid decline in estimated welfare program participation. Over 55% of those on AFDC were estimated to exit within 5 years, and 80% within 10 years, after age 28.

Projections had to be made for participation in other welfare programs as well. For those receiving AFDC, we assumed participation in the food stamp and Medicaid programs. A few persons not receiving AFDC at age 27 participated in other programs, such as GA, food stamps, and Medicaid (or the comparable state program). Discontinuation of the GA program eliminated the need for us to project GA payments, but participation projections were still made for these persons for food stamps and Medicaid. For lack of better information, we made the same assumption for these programs as for AFDC — that the probability of exit was 15% each year through age 50.

Welfare payment amounts for each month of projected participation were estimated as follows: We based estimates of AFDC payments on 1991 Michigan average monthly payments to families by number of dependents. To estimate the number of dependents, the projected age of each child born up to the time of the interview was used; no further births were projected. For AFDC participants and others, we estimated the size of food stamp and medical assistance payments by using the same assumptions and estimates employed to estimate the size of payments from these programs prior to age 27.

The payment estimations that we produced by combining projected rates of welfare participation with estimated monthly payment amounts almost certainly underestimated study participants' welfare payments after age 27. Our method of projecting rates of participation ignored (1) those who leave welfare by age 27 but reenter later, (2) those who leave after age 27 and reenter, and (3) those who enter for the first time after age 27. These limitations are hardly trivial — 30% of all first-time AFDC recipients are over age 30 when they begin receiving AFDC (Committee on Ways and Means, 1991). Half of all those who leave poverty become poor again within 4 years (Stevens, 1994). However, we concluded that better projections for new entry and reentry could not be developed, because of the lack of information about the relevant populations (e.g., the rate and timing of entry/reentry by age, duration of welfare participation, average payment amount). Our simple projections could at least, with some confidence, be considered underestimates of the welfare participation of both the program and the no-program group.

In an attempt to develop an alternative procedure for projecting welfare payments based strictly on data for the High/Scope Perry preschool sample, we estimated regression equations relating payment amounts to age. Although we tried a variety of functional forms in an attempt to produce a good fit, the estimated equations fit the data poorly and severely underestimated payments at ages 25 to 27. In addition, the regressions produced estimates for later years that seemed grossly inconsistent with national data on patterns of AFDC participation by age. Thus, regression equations estimated for the sample data through age 27 did not offer a plausible alternative and were not considered further.

Current welfare reform efforts raise questions about whether the benefits from a preschool program's effects on welfare might be lower in the future. If welfare reform that is enacted actually *succeeds* in reducing the use of welfare programs, preschool program benefits from effects on welfare use might be lower. Although the political future of welfare reform and its success are difficult to predict, it seems unlikely that costs will decline substantially. Even the most conservative budget projections predict that Medicaid spending will increase. Federal subsidies for child care that enables parents to leave welfare could eat up much of the savings, as could increased use of the earned-income tax credit. Nevertheless, our estimates of benefits from welfare reduction are so conservative that they are unlikely to overestimate benefits under any conceivable welfare reform.

Summary of Effects on Welfare Payments and Costs to Society

Table 26 reports study participants' estimated welfare payments before and after age 27; Table 27 reports the estimated per person effects of the preschool program on payments (per person reductions in welfare payments) discounted at various rates. Because welfare payments are transfer payments (taking money from one set of people and giving it to another), the figures reported in Table 27 are not estimates of the benefits to society as a whole. The societal costs of welfare programs are limited to the programs' administrative costs. Over the relevant period, these administrative costs have ranged from 10% to 15% of payment amounts, reaching the higher figure only in recent years. Therefore the benefits to society as a whole from the High/Scope Perry Preschool program's effects on welfare participation were estimated to equal 10% of the welfare payment reductions in Table 27. Of course, even the differences in payment amounts are smaller than what

Table 26

ESTIMATED PER PERSON WELFARE PAYMENTS BY PROGRAM ATTENDANCE AND GENDER (IN REAL 1992 DOLLARS, UNDISCOUNTED)

Source	Through Age 27	Beyond Age 27	Lifetime
Program females	$26,272	$13,570	$39,842
No-program females	29,387	15,666	45,053
Program males	2,399	560	2,959
No-program males	7,118	782	7,900

Table 27

PRESENT VALUE OF ESTIMATED PRESCHOOL PROGRAM EFFECT
ON WELFARE PAYMENTS (IN REAL 1992 DOLLARS)

Discount Rate	Reduction in Payments to Males	Reduction in Payments to Females	Average Reduction in Payments
Discounted at 0%			
Through age 27	$4,719	$3,115	$3,917
Beyond age 27	222	2,096	1,159
Total	4,941	5,211	5,076
Total discounted at 3%	2,727	2,580	2,653
Total discounted at 5%	1,833	1,811	1,822
Total discounted at 7%	1,278	1,352	1,315

some might have expected, considering the effects of the preschool program on earnings. However, an increase in very low-level earnings does not necessarily have much of an impact on welfare program eligibility. Moreover, there is some evidence of substantial underreporting of earnings by welfare program participants, so welfare payments and earnings are not as strongly related in practice as in principle (Jencks & Edin, 1990; Lemieux, Fortin, & Frechette, 1994).

IV Benefit-Cost Summary and Sensitivity Analyses

All of the estimated costs and benefits from previous chapters are brought together in this chapter to assess the High/Scope Perry Preschool program's total economic impact on society and to show how that impact is distributed within society. In addition, this chapter reports sensitivity analyses that examine the effects of variations in key assumptions and the omission of benefits for which an economic value could not be estimated. As will be explained, the assumptions and omissions of benefits in this study seem likely to lead to underestimation rather than overestimation of benefits. As a result, the conclusions of this economic analysis are quite insensitive to plausible changes in assumptions.

Aggregation of Costs and Benefits

The primary purpose of this benefit-cost analysis is to determine whether the High/Scope Perry Preschool program could be considered a sound investment. The way to assess this is to ask whether the net effect (the present value of benefits minus costs) is positive. Table 28 (on the next page) and Tables 31 and 32 (on pages 77 and 78), in which the present value of program effects is calculated using real rates of 3%, 5%, and 7%, respectively, give the answer to that question. The "bottom line" in all of these calculations is positive and quite large relative to cost. Thus, there is a substantial margin for error. Based on this economic analysis, we can say that the gains to society from investing in the High/Scope Perry Preschool program were substantial. Although estimates of the present value of program effects are not available for most other government programs, it seems likely that a substantial number of sizeable federal and state programs that compete for government funding could not be shown to produce such a positive benefit (see, for example, the many examples provided by Gross, 1992). It is safe to conclude that the High/Scope Perry Preschool program was a good investment for society.

Note that the estimated present value of per child benefits, which, discounted at 3%, equals $108,002, is substantially different from the simple sum of benefits that one often sees reported for programs described in the media. The *undiscounted* sum of estimated benefits from the High/Scope Perry Preschool program is more than twice as large as the discounted sum — $242,646 per child.

Distribution of Costs and Benefits

In the case of the High/Scope Perry Preschool program, costs and benefits accrued to two groups: program *participants* — children in very low-income African-American families — and the *general public* — who are taxpayers and crime victims. This division, which we use in all of the tables reporting aggregate costs and benefits, is conceptual rather than literal; instead of constructing distinct groups of real persons, it separates people into two groups based on their roles. The program participants are taxpayers and crime vic-

Table 28

PRESCHOOL PROGRAM'S ESTIMATED EFFECTS PER PROGRAM PARTICIPANT
(PRESENT VALUE, 1992 DOLLARS DISCOUNTED AT 3%)

Effect[a]	For Participant Only	For General Public (Taxpayers/ Crime Victims)	Total (For Society as a Whole)
Measured effect			
Child care	$ 738	$ 0	$ 738
K–12 education	0	6,872	6,872
Adult education	0	283	283
College[b]	0	−868	−868
Earnings[c]	10,270	4,228	14,498
Crime	0	49,044	49,044
Welfare	−2,193	2,412	219
Total measured	$ 8,815	$61,972	$ 70,786
Projected effect			
Earnings	11,215	4,618	15,833
Crime	0	21,337	21,337
Welfare	−460	506	46
Total projected	$10,755	$26,461	$ 37,216
Total measured & projected	$19,570	$88,433	$108,002
Cost of preschool program	0	−12,356	−12,356
Net benefit	$19,570	$76,077	$ 95,646

[a]Costs appear as negative numbers; benefits appear as positive numbers.

[b]Some small portion of college costs is likely to have been borne by the participants, but this could not be estimated from the available information.

[c]The benefits reported under *earnings* include all costs paid by the employer to hire a program participant. Allocation between participants and taxpayers assumes that the marginal tax rate is 25%, that the value of fringe benefits to the employee equals 10% of salary, and that other costs to the employer equal 10% of salary.

tims, too, but they are so small a part of those groups that their share of taxpayer and crime victim benefits can safely be ignored. This conceptual division also captures the economist's distinction between direct benefits and indirect benefits, which are sometimes called *externalities* or *spillover effects*. The benefits to program participants are the direct benefits of the program. The benefits to taxpayers are the indirect benefits, or externalities, produced as a byproduct of the direct effects on the participants.

In most cases it was a relatively simple matter to divide the costs and benefits into those that accrued to participants and those that accrued to the general public. However, in the case of the costs of higher education and earnings benefits, it was necessary to make some rough assumptions. All of the participants who went to college enrolled in public institutions that were highly subsidized, and most probably obtained additional direct financial aid. Those who attended college would have had some out-of-pocket costs, but those costs were likely to be such a small portion of total costs that they could safely be ignored. (The indirect costs of higher education in the form of foregone earnings would be more substantial, but these were accounted for in our estimation of program effects on earnings). Based on studies of tax incidence by level of personal income, we assumed that the marginal tax rate applicable to the earnings benefit produced by the preschool program was 25% (Fullerton & Rogers, 1993; Pechman, 1985). There is obviously some uncertainty here, particularly because of the extent to which persons at various income levels can conceal income. For example, compared with the no-program group, the program group had more formal employment in regular jobs at larger companies, so it would have been more difficult for them to avoid income and Social Security taxes (Lemieux et al., 1994). In the case of fringe benefits and other costs paid by the employer, we assumed that half of these (equal to 10% of salary) accrue to employees and half to taxpayers and others (U.S. Bureau of Labor Statistics, 1992; Woodbury & Hamermesh, 1992). The rationale for this is that roughly half of these costs are taxes and mandated insurance fees paid by employers.

Both direct and indirect benefits were positive and large relative to costs. The estimates of positive and large direct benefits indicate that the preschool program achieved its primary goal of significantly improving the lives of children who grew up in poverty. At a discount rate of 3%, the estimated direct benefits by themselves exceeded the program cost (Table 28). When we use higher discount rates to calculate present value of benefits, direct benefits no longer exceed the program cost (Tables 31–35 on pp. 77–81). But it must be taken into account that the dollar value of some important direct benefits could not be estimated. For example, the increased school success of participants undoubtedly improved the quality of their lives during their school years, but no dollar value for this benefit is included in the analysis. Similarly, the increased status and enjoyment from better jobs was not included in the analysis. It is not unreasonable to suppose that the omitted intangible benefits to participants were substantial enough to tip the scales in favor of direct benefits, even when we use a 7% discount rate to calculate present value.

Estimated indirect benefits were substantially larger than estimated direct benefits. This means that the taxpayers who financed the program obtained an impressive return on their investment. Moreover, the substantial tangible benefits to taxpayers begin to accrue relatively early. Most of the estimated monetary gains accrue to the general public through reduced costs of crime; these are followed in importance by reduced costs for schooling and increased tax payments due to the higher earnings of program participants. Transfer payments such as welfare payments are much more important from the perspective of *taxpayers* than from the perspective of *society as a whole*, because for *taxpayers*, reductions in both payments and administrative costs are counted as benefits. For *society as a whole*, only the reduction in administrative costs is a benefit. Thus, overall, the estimated value of reductions in welfare usage remains small relative to other major benefits.

There are two important public policy implications of these distributional findings. First, the preschool program appears to be a social program from which everybody wins. Most people would find this to be a fair interpretation of results, and therefore such a program is likely to be popular politically. Second, the distribution of benefits offers a strong rationale for public funding, because low-income families do not have the resources to purchase high-quality preschool programs that could be expected to produce these long-term benefits. At the same time, the general public has substantial economic incentive to provide such programs or to make funds available to enable low-income families to purchase such programs. The substantial direct benefits to the participants provide an economic incentive for low-income families to spend such funds wisely — provided they have reasonably adequate information on the costs and benefits of various preschool programs.

Gender Differences

It was not surprising to find differences in the ways that preschool education affected the lives of male versus female participants. There are considerable differences in the behavior, expectations, aspirations, and experiences of men and women with respect to education, employment, family formation, and household activities. Thus, even if the preschool program had produced identical immediate effects on girls and boys, the long-term consequences or manifestations of those effects could be expected to differ. As will be seen, the pattern of benefits does vary greatly by gender. However, estimated total benefits to society are virtually identical for males and females. Thus, the conclusion that the preschool program was a sound social investment is equally valid for males and females.

Tables 29 and 30 display the preschool program's estimated effects for females only and for males only, respectively. Note that one of the largest gender differences in program effects is in the category of *earnings*. Estimated earnings benefits are much greater for females than for males. This difference in earnings can be traced to the preschool program's much larger impact on females' educational attainment. This in turn was one of the factors leading to much larger estimated earnings for females (the larger earnings estimate was also partly due to the approach used to project earnings). The other noteworthy gender differences were larger education and crime cost savings for males. In the case of education, this appears to be largely because of the greater educational attainment of program females. In the case of crime, the difference may be attributed to the greater opportunities for improvement in male behavior. For example, by age 28, the estimated *reduction* in arrests for males was as large as the total number of arrests for no-program females. Reducing females' crime costs to zero would not have produced benefits as large as those estimated for males.

Overall, from the perspective of program participants, Tables 29 and 30 show males benefiting much less than females. This female advantage is primarily due to their estimated earnings increase based on the preschool program's effect on their educational attainment. Recall that given the program's lack of effect on males' educational attainment, we projected no earnings benefits for them beyond age 27. Of course, even when we compare earnings estimates only through age 27, males still appear to be at a disadvantage. However, some caution is warranted by the monthly earnings estimates obtained from the age-27 interview, which indicated that the preschool program had a larger effect on male earnings than on female earnings (Schweinhart et al., 1993). Possibly the preschool program had an impact on male

Table 29

PRESCHOOL PROGRAM'S ESTIMATED EFFECTS PER FEMALE PROGRAM PARTICIPANT
(PRESENT VALUE, 1992 DOLLARS DISCOUNTED AT 3%)

Effect[a]	For Participant Only	For General Public (Taxpayers/ Crime Victims)	Total (For Society as a Whole)
Measured effect			
Child care	$ 738	$ 0	$ 738
K–12 education	0	4,282	4,282
Adult education	0	418	418
College[b]	0	−2,228	−2,228
Earnings[c]	16,818	6,925	23,743
Crime	0	34,587	34,587
Welfare	−1,788	1,967	179
Total measured	**$15,768**	**$45,951**	**$ 61,719**
Projected effect			
Earnings	22,432	9,236	31,668
Crime	0	15,329	15,329
Welfare	−850	935	85
Total projected	**$21,582**	**$25,500**	**$ 47,082**
Total measured & projected	$37,350	$71,451	$108,801
Cost of preschool program	0	−12,356	−12,356
Net benefit	$37,350	$59,095	$ 96,445

[a]Costs appear as negative numbers; benefits appear as positive numbers.

[b]Some small portion of college costs is likely to have been borne by the participants, but this could not be estimated from the available information.

[c]The benefits reported under *earnings* include all costs paid by the employer to hire a program participant. Allocation between participants and taxpayers assumes that the marginal tax rate is 25%, that the value of fringe benefits to the employee equals 10% of salary, and that other costs to the employer equal 10% of salary.

earnings that the benefit-cost analysis did not take into account (for example, an impact related to their decreased involvement in crime). Although the estimated gender differences do not lessen the desirability of preschool programs as a social investment, they indicate the need for further research on the nature and extent of gender differences in effects of preschool education.

Sensitivity Analyses

All of the results presented to this point have been based on a single analysis with one set of assumptions in which the only variation was the choice of 3%, 5%, or 7% as the annual discount rate. On the whole, this set of assump-

Table 30

PRESCHOOL PROGRAM'S ESTIMATED EFFECTS PER MALE PROGRAM PARTICIPANT
(PRESENT VALUE, 1992 DOLLARS DISCOUNTED AT 3%)

Effect[a]	For Participant Only	For General Public (Taxpayers/ Crime Victims)	Total (For Society as a Whole)
Measured effect			
Child care	$ 738	$ 0	$ 738
K–12 education	0	9,461	9,461
Adult education	0	147	147
College[b]	0	492	492
Earnings[c]	3,720	1,532	5,252
Crime	0	63,500	63,500
Welfare	−2,698	2,968	270
Total measured	**$1,760**	**$ 78,100**	**$ 79,860**
Projected effect			
Earnings	0	0	0
Crime	0	27,344	27,344
Welfare	−91	100	9
Total projected	**$ −91**	**$ 27,444**	**$ 27,353**
Total measured & projected	$1,669	$105,544	$107,213
Cost of preschool program	0	−12,356	−12,356
Net benefit	$1,669	$ 93,188	$ 94,857

[a]Costs appear as negative numbers; benefits appear as positive numbers.

[b]Some small portion of college costs is likely to have been borne by the participants, but this could not be estimated from the available information.

[c]The benefits reported under *earnings* include all costs paid by the employer to hire a program participant. Allocation between participants and taxpayers assumes that the marginal tax rate is 25%, that the value of fringe benefits to the employee equals 10% of salary, and that other costs to the employer equal 10% of salary.

tions is reasonable and cautious. When choosing between equally reasonable assumptions — one of which risked overestimation and the other, underestimation of the benefits of the program — we presumed in favor of underestimation. Errors in our underlying assumptions are therefore likely to lead to underestimation of the preschool program's benefits, so this benefit-cost analysis can be considered to produce a lower-bound estimate of total benefits. In this section of the monograph, we investigate in some detail the extent to which the analysis results may be affected by key assumptions and other limitations. We also seek to identify assumptions that might have to hold in the future if large-scale efforts at preschool education for disadvantaged children are to obtain the same benefits estimated here.

Before presenting specific sensitivity analyses, we should note that the results of this benefit-cost analysis depend on the particular political, economic, and social environments in which the High/Scope Perry Preschool program was implemented. For the most part, there is no way to investigate the impact of any variations in these ecological characteristics. Practically speaking, this means that in generalizing the results, we should recognize that there are likely to be important interactions between preschool programs and the families, schools, and neighborhoods in which children live. At present, the impact of these interactions can only be estimated based on theory and a review of the evidence from other preschool studies. For example, *one* reason that studies have found preschool programs to vary in their apparent effects on special education placements and grade retentions is that school districts vary in their policies and practices with respect to special education and retention (Barnett, 1992). Where very few children are placed in special education or retained in grade, little effect on these outcomes is possible, although there may be less visible impacts on tracking, ability grouping, and performance. As another example, for various reasons, extremely poor "ghetto" neighborhoods of large cities may present greater obstacles to producing persistent improvements in educational and social outcomes than do other types of neighborhoods; however, the poorest neighborhoods may present greater opportunities as well (Anderson, 1990; Jargowsky & Bane, 1991; Jencks, 1991; Wilson, 1987).

In some communities it may be necessary to take steps to ensure that the elementary schools children attend are good enough to support the gains that children make in preschool programs. Alternatively, it may be that if preschool programs provide children with sufficiently large "head starts," children's early gains may be largely self-sustaining through the efforts of the children and their families, even in the context of exceptionally poor elementary schools.

No doubt the reader can supply further examples of important contextual variables. The point is that some thought must be given to these contexts when generalizing the results of the benefit-cost analysis and planning preschool policy, and no one should expect to obtain in each and every time and place exactly the same benefits that are estimated for this program. Benefits in each category estimated here may be higher or lower for other program implementations. The following sensitivity analyses provide some confidence that benefit estimates could shrink considerably without altering the conclusion that preschool programs are a sound investment.

Effect of the Initial Group Difference in Maternal Employment

The only apparent flaw in the initial equivalence of program and no-program groups was that program-group members had significantly fewer mothers in paid employment than did no-program-group members (9% vs. 31%). It is possible that this difference between the program and no-program groups on mother's employment at entry could bias the estimation of program effects and thus the results of the benefit-cost analysis. Therefore we conducted two types of statistical analyses to investigate the relationship between *mother's employment at entry* and outcome variables important in the benefit-cost analysis. First, we estimated correlations between mother's employment and outcome variables, to examine the strength of association. We estimated these correlations both for the full sample and for males and females separately. Finding no significant correlation between outcome variables and mother's employment would mean that the latter is not a potential source of bias. Second, we estimated means and percentages of the outcome variables for those with and without employed mothers at study entry, to investigate the size of the effect of mother's employment.

The outcome variables examined for the sample were these: (1) *years of educational attainment by age 27*, (2) *high school graduation* (yes or no), (3) *years of special education with a classification as mentally impaired*, (4) *number of arrests*, (5) *number of arrests as an adult*, (6) *number of months on welfare in the past 10 years*, (7) *number of months on welfare in the past 5 years*, (8) *whether or not the person had ever received welfare as an adult*, (9) *earnings from employment in the past year*, and (10) *earnings from employment in the past month*. For none of these 10 critical variables did we find a relationship that would have biased the economic analysis in the direction of overestimating the benefits of the preschool program. Table A1 in the Appendix presents the complete results of the correlation analyses.

The correlation analyses reveal that the initial difference on mother's employment outside the home can be expected to have only minimal effects on the results, and these effects tend to bias the benefit-cost analysis in the direction of underestimating benefits for males. All of the estimated correlations are modest. Only three outcome variables were found to have statistically significant correlations with mother's employment (using the liberal criterion of $p < .10$), and the effects appear to be limited to males. Males with employed mothers were somewhat less likely to be placed in classes for children with mental impairment and had somewhat higher education levels as adults.

The results of the *t*-tests of mean differences between the mother-employed and mother-not-employed groups were similar. The only differences found to be statistically significant (again using $p < .10$) were in the direction of more favorable outcomes for participants whose mothers were employed at study entry. Two differences were found for males: For those with mothers employed at study entry, (1) educational attainment was higher, and (2) number of months on welfare in the last 10 years was lower. One difference was found for females: For those with mothers employed at study entry, number of adult arrests was lower. These differences are large enough to be meaningful (for example, 49% vs. 77% for male high school graduation, and 1.0 crimes vs. 0.1 crime per adult female), but because the number of cases involved is so small, the total effect on the results is quite small. A shift of only 10% of the cases would have been sufficient to perfectly equate the groups on maternal employment.

Alternative Assumptions for Benefit Projections

To project benefits beyond age 27, it was necessary to make a considerable number of assumptions. Compared with other reasonable assumptions, the assumptions used tended to produce lower projections of benefits from increased earnings, from reduced welfare program participation, and from reductions in crime. In the cases of crime and welfare, because of lack of data, specific alternative assumptions are difficult to specify. As demonstrated in the next two sections, the size of the potential bias resulting from the more questionable assumptions for welfare and crime reductions seems likely to be small relative to total estimated benefits. For earnings, a case can be made for specific alternative assumptions. One set of these alternative earnings assumptions taken together might increase earnings projections sufficiently to raise total estimated benefits by 10% to 20%.

Crime cost reductions. In projecting the costs of crime, we assumed that for each treatment-by-gender group, the costs of crime after age 28 could be predicted from the costs of crime through age 28 and national age-arrest profiles by gender. In other words, as explained in Chapter 3 on p. 55, because 60% of all arrests occur by age 28, we considered study participants' crime costs through age 28 to represent 60% of their lifetime crime costs. We chose this procedure for its simplicity, but the procedure does not take into account the fact that one might expect a person's propensity for crimes and arrests to decline with the length of time since a person's last incident. Because the program group, compared with the no-program group, seemed to have had fewer and less serious arrests in the period just before age 28, a strictly proportional projection of their post-age-28 crime based on their *entire* period up to age 28 may tend to underestimate the difference in post-age-28 crime costs between the program and no-program groups. However, given the uncertainty involved in this projection of future reductions in crime costs in the first place, there seems little point in trying to fine-tune it without having better information on patterns of crime. Moreover, fine-tuning would have little impact on the results. For example, if the projected costs of crime for preschool program participants beyond age 28 were reduced by 25%, this would increase the total projected crime benefits by less than 15%, and the total estimated benefits would increase by only 3%.

Welfare cost reductions. Although the assumptions we employed to project welfare benefits were fairly crude and probably tended to underestimate future cost reductions due to the preschool program, it seems unlikely that this is a source of serious underestimation of program impact. Our most important conservative welfare assumptions were that only those receiving welfare at age 27 would receive welfare after age 27 and that anyone leaving welfare after age 27 would never return. Clearly, these are unrealistic assumptions, but the available national data did not support any reasonable alternatives. One alternative would be to base post-age-27 projections on the sample data through age 27 and assume no decrease in the program and no-program groups' welfare usage differential after age 27 (this would require that Michigan reinstate General Assistance for males). This alternative assumption would produce a large *percentage* increase in projected welfare cost savings from preschool programs. However, the *absolute size* of the increase in estimated net social benefits would be negligible. For example, discounted at 3% (the rate at which the alternative assumption would have the largest impact), the alternative assumption would increase projected benefits to *society as a whole* by less than $200 per participant. Even the effect on projected benefits to *taxpayers* would be less than $2,000 per participant, which is less than 2% of estimated *total* benefits.

Earnings. Three of the major assumptions we used to project earnings may be considered unduly conservative. The first of these assumptions was that productivity growth would be zero over the next four decades.

Although experience in the 1980s for the economy as a whole might justify this assumption as a lower-bound estimate, it is unduly pessimistic in light of longer historical trends for the United States and represents a future for which the nation is, to say the least, unprepared. To examine the limiting effect of this assumption, we projected earnings based on the assumption of 2% annual productivity growth. This new assumption generated earnings projections that were considerably larger. The undiscounted projected earnings benefit under this assumption was roughly $23,000 higher per person. This would increase the present value of projected earnings by roughly $8,000 per participant at a 3% discount rate, $5,000 at 5%, or $2,000 at 7%.

A second conservative assumption of our analysis was that female labor force participation would remain at the levels implied by the national cross-sectional earnings-and-education data that we used to project study participants' post-age-27 earnings. However, the women in the High/Scope Perry Preschool study, who were born between 1958 and 1962, are likely to have considerably higher labor force participation rates (and thus earnings) than the cohorts in the national data (Olsen, 1994). The women in the national data, who were used to project study participants' earnings to ages 40, 50, and 60, were born in roughly 1950, 1940, and 1930, respectively, and therefore belong to age-cohorts that have had lower labor force participation rates. At age 27, the employment rate of program females was 80%, which is much higher than the employment rate of all African-American women (54% in 1991). In fact, the program group's employment rate is even higher than the national average for their age cohort, because the labor force participation rate of black women aged 25 to 29 was 72% in 1988, and unemployment probably reduced this employment rate to about 66% in 1992. Thus, it seems likely that our use of the labor force participation rates implicit in the national cross-sectional data tended to result in underestimation of the preschool program's effect on lifetime earnings.

The third conservative assumption we made was that because there was no effect on male educational attainment by age 27, there would be no post-age-27 earnings benefits for program males. However, the earnings data from age 19 to age 27 consistently favor the program males. Based on actual earnings through age 27, one would predict an earnings advantage for program males beyond age 27. Unfortunately, because they produced estimated regression equations that fit the data poorly, attempts to project future earnings based on the pattern through age 27 were not satisfying. A crude alternative would have been to assume that the proportion of earnings and related benefits received beyond age 27 was the same for males as for females. This would have increased projected per person earnings benefits for males by roughly $5,000 (discounted at 3%) to $1,000 (discounted at 7%).

Omitted Benefits

It is generally easier to estimate all of the costs than to estimate all of the benefits of educational and social programs, and the High/Scope Perry Preschool program is no exception to this rule. Many of the benefits identified in this analysis (in Table 2 on page 9) were estimated incompletely or not at all. In some cases, the High/Scope Perry Preschool study did not produce estimates of the underlying effects (for example, effects on siblings). In other cases, effects (such as the effect of more enjoyable school experiences) were estimated, but reasonable estimates of their economic value could not be developed. The most relevant omitted benefits are the "productivity in household activities" benefits that previous economic research has found to result from improvements in education and cognitive development. These include improved financial and household management and the family's increased productivity with respect to nonmarket goods, including health, longevity, and child quality (Haveman & Wolfe, 1984; Jorgenson & Fraumeni, 1989).

The High/Scope Perry Preschool study (Barnett, 1993a; Schweinhart et al., 1993) provides some evidence that the preschool program's long-term effects included some of the household production benefits just listed. For example, the program group was found to be more likely to own their homes and to have two cars. This may be regarded as evidence that the program group members were better able to manage their financial affairs, although an alternative explanation is that the program group members had better access to credit because they had higher and more stable earnings. In the case of health, data from participants' self-reports of health status and illness showed no evidence of benefits. The program group did report more hospitalization, suggesting that they had greater access to health care (perhaps because more had insurance through employment), which might improve their long-term health outcomes.

Possibly age 27 was too soon for any health differences to have been noticed in this study, given the small sample-sizes. Nevertheless, health benefits should be expected in the future. National data indicate that mortality rates for African-American men and women aged 25 to 64 decline sharply as education and income rise; for example, age-adjusted mortality rates for those with at least some college are roughly half the rates for high school dropouts (Pappas, Queen, Hadden, & Fisher, 1993). In addition, for African-American men and women, higher education levels have been found to be associated with more disability-free years of life in the years beyond retirement — a period not considered in this benefit-cost analysis (Guralnik, Land, Blazer, Fillenbaum, & Branch, 1993).

Benefits to the children of the program group would be expected to result from improved management of fertility, better parenting, and improved family economic circumstances. The study provides evidence that the preschool program produced substantial effects on these determinants of children's well-being, though reductions in births to teenagers and reductions in out-of-wedlock births were found only for females, for whom the small sample-size creates problems for precisely estimating effects (Schweinhart et al., 1993). The increased percentage of children living with two parents, by itself, would be expected to produce substantial benefits for children. Expected benefits for the next generation include improved birth outcomes and early cognitive development; reduced risk of abuse, failure to thrive, and accidental injury; and increased educational achievement and attainment and their attendant benefits (Baumeister, Kupstas, & Klindworth, 1991; Daniel, Hampton, & Newberger, 1983; Datcher-Loury, 1989; Hack et al., 1991; Milne, Myers, Rosenthal, & Ginsburg, 1986;).

In addition to the omitted benefits discussed thus far, there were some cases in which the intrinsic value of benefits could not be estimated although their instrumental value to the participants or society could. The two most important categories of these omitted benefits are (a) increased success in school and (b) increased success in work and family life. The program group was more successful in school academically, and there are indications that their school experiences were more enjoyable socially as well (Berrueta-Clement et al., 1984; Schweinhart & Weikart, 1980). Both children and parents in the program group indicated that they felt better about their school experiences, and at age 27 the program group felt more confident in their ability to work or study hard all day (Schweinhart et al., 1993). The achievement data indicate that program children learned more. Improved employment and earnings increased the socioeconomic status and economic self-sufficiency of those who attended the preschool program. A substantially lower arrest rate probably contributed to increased well-being and status. Females in the program group were more likely be married at age 27 and had obtained fewer abortions. Whatever one's view about abortion, it is surely a benefit that fewer were deemed to be necessary.

The foregoing description suggests the extent to which benefit estimation falls short of capturing the full economic value of the High/Scope Perry Preschool program's long-term effects. Although the extent of underestimation cannot be assessed with precision, clearly it is nontrivial. The types of effects for which benefit estimates could not be produced are no less important than those for which dollar values were estimated. Conceivably, the value of the omitted benefits alone might offset the cost of the preschool program. As one test of this proposition, readers might consider whether, for their own children, they would be willing to pay the cost of the High/Scope Perry Preschool program to produce only the *omitted* benefits described here.

Alternative Discount Rates

The uncertainty regarding the appropriate discount rate was noted from the start and was reflected in our use of a range of discount rates in all of the analyses. Because some economists would argue for the use of discount rates even higher than the 3% to 7% range employed to this point, the effects of higher rates are investigated here. (Others would argue for lower rates, but lower rates would only increase our confidence that net benefits were positive.) Recall that using the 3% discount rate, the analysis results were those shown in Table 28 on p. 66 (results of the overall analysis), Table 29 on p. 69 (results for females), and Table 30 on p. 70 (results for males). Tables 31 through 35 on the next five pages present the results of the analysis using real discount rates of 5%, 7%, 9%, 10%, and 11%, respectively. The higher rates approximate real pre-tax marginal rates of return in the private sector, which is the rate recommended by some, under the assumption that expenditure for the program displaces private-sector investment (Lind, 1982; Stockfisch, 1982).

As can be seen from the tables, the estimated net effect remains positive at all of these discount rates. Discounted at 11%, the present value of the estimated net benefit is an order of magnitude lower than when it is dis-

Table 31

PRESCHOOL PROGRAM'S ESTIMATED EFFECTS PER PROGRAM PARTICIPANT
(PRESENT VALUE, 1992 DOLLARS DISCOUNTED AT 5%)

Effect[a]	For Participant Only	For General Public (Taxpayers/ Crime Victims)	Total (For Society as a Whole)
Measured effect			
Child care	$ 722	$ 0	$ 722
K–12 education	0	5,575	5,575
Adult education	0	188	188
College[b]	0	-590	-590
Earnings[c]	6,626	2,728	9,354
Crime	0	33,516	33,516
Welfare	-1,566	1,723	157
Total measured	$ 5,782	$43,140	$48,922
Projected effect			
Earnings	4,911	2,023	6,934
Crime	0	11,214	11,214
Welfare	-254	279	25
Total projected	$ 4,657	$13,516	$18,173
Total measured & projected	$10,439	$56,656	$67,095
Cost of preschool program	0	-12,022	-12,022
Net benefit	$10,439	$44,634	$55,073

[a]Costs appear as negative numbers; benefits appear as positive numbers.

[b]Some small portion of college costs is likely to have been borne by the participants, but this could not be estimated from the available information.

[c]The benefits reported under *earnings* include all costs paid by the employer to hire a program participant. Allocation between participants and taxpayers assumes that the marginal tax rate is 25%, that the value of fringe benefits to the employee equals 10% of salary, and that other costs to the employer equal 10% of salary.

counted at 3% (see again Table 28, p. 66), but it remains positive and substantial. Thus, the conclusion that the High/Scope Perry Preschool program represents a sound public investment on purely economic grounds is quite unaffected by a wide selection of discount rates.

General Robustness With Respect to Changes in Magnitudes of Benefits

Even if one accepts the basic assumptions underlying benefit estimation, there is still room for doubt about the accuracy of the estimation. The nonmonetary effects estimates underlying the economic-value estimates are themselves subject to some uncertainty, and additional uncertainty is intro-

Table 32

PRESCHOOL PROGRAM'S ESTIMATED EFFECTS PER PROGRAM PARTICIPANT
(PRESENT VALUE, 1992 DOLLARS DISCOUNTED AT 7%)

Effect[a]	For Participant Only	For General Public (Taxpayers/ Crime Victims)	Total (For Society as a Whole)
Measured effect			
Child care	$ 702	$ 0	$ 702
K–12 education	0	4,441	4,441
Adult education	0	127	127
College[b]	0	−354	−354
Earnings[c]	4,320	1,778	6,098
Crime	0	23,238	23,238
Welfare	−1,172	1,289	117
Total measured	**$3,850**	**$30,519**	**$34,369**
Projected effect			
Earnings	2,421	997	3,418
Crime	0	6,055	6,055
Welfare	−142	156	14
Total projected	**$2,279**	**$ 7,208**	**$ 9,487**
Total measured & projected	$6,129	$37,727	$43,856
Cost of preschool program	0	−11,705	−11,705
Net benefit	**$6,129**	**$26,002**	**$32,151**

[a]Costs appear as negative numbers; benefits appear as positive numbers.

[b]Some small portion of college costs is likely to have been borne by the participants, but this could not be estimated from the available information.

[c]The benefits reported under *earnings* include all costs paid by the employer to hire a program participant. Allocation between participants and taxpayers assumes that the marginal tax rate is 25%, that the value of fringe benefits to the employee equals 10% of salary, and that other costs to the employer equal 10% of salary.

duced by our use of estimated values from other sources in our calculations. When these estimated values are used to project benefits into the future, even more uncertainty is introduced. Of course, the uncertainties are not all in the same direction, and the true value of benefits could be either higher or lower. However, in light of the results, the possibility that benefit estimates have been biased upward is our greatest concern. This section investigates the consequences of reducing the estimated value of benefits to determine how much error can be tolerated without producing an erroneous conclusion about the preschool program as a sound investment.

If discount rates of 3% to 7% are used, the results are highly robust with respect to errors in benefit estimation. When 3% is used as the discount rate, even reducing benefits to one eighth of their estimated value would not change the basic result. When 7% is used as the discount rate, benefits could be divided by 3 and still exceed costs. At any rate up to 7%,

Table 33

PRESCHOOL PROGRAM'S ESTIMATED EFFECTS PER PROGRAM PARTICIPANT
(PRESENT VALUE, 1992 DOLLARS DISCOUNTED AT 9%)

Effect[a]	For Participant Only	For General Public (Taxpayers/ Crime Victims)	Total (For Society as a Whole)
Measured effect			
Child care	$ 691	$ 0	$ 691
K–12 education	0	3,609	3,609
Adult education	0	111	111
College[b]	0	-339	-339
Earnings[c]	3,378	1,391	4,769
Crime	0	16,341	16,341
Welfare	-774	851	77
Total measured	**$3,295**	**$21,964**	**$25,259**
Projected effect			
Earnings	1,217	501	1,718
Crime	0	2,731	2,731
Welfare	-84	92	8
Total projected	**$1,133**	**$ 3,324**	**$ 4,457**
Total measured & projected	**$4,428**	**$25,288**	**$29,716**
Cost of preschool program	0	-11,399	-11,399
Net benefit	**$4,428**	**$13,889**	**$18,317**

[a] Costs appear as negative numbers; benefits appear as positive numbers.

[b] Some small portion of college costs is likely to have been borne by the participants, but this could not be estimated from the available information.

[c] The benefits reported under *earnings* include all costs paid by the employer to hire a program participant. Allocation between participants and taxpayers assumes that the marginal tax rate is 25%, that the value of fringe benefits to the employee equals 10% of salary, and that other costs to the employer equal 10% of salary.

all child care, welfare, and crime reduction benefits could be set equal to zero, and benefits would still exceed costs.

Further sensitivity analyses were conducted using two very high real discount rates, 9% and 11%. Use of these rates, which encompass the upper range of rates employed, makes these further analyses quite conservative.

When we use a 9% discount rate (Table 33), it is clear that extremely large and pervasive decreases in our benefit estimates would be required to alter the final conclusion. The most dramatic illustration of this is that if all measured benefits estimated through age 27 are reduced by half, and all benefit projections beyond age 27 are set equal to zero, the present value of the estimated net benefit remains positive. Moreover, any one of the benefit estimates can be set equal to zero without jeopardizing the finding of a positive net benefit.

When we use an 11% discount rate (Table 35), the results cannot be

Table 34

PRESCHOOL PROGRAM'S ESTIMATED EFFECTS PER PROGRAM PARTICIPANT
(PRESENT VALUE, 1992 DOLLARS DISCOUNTED AT 10%)

Effect[a]	For Participant Only	For General Public (Taxpayers/ Crime Victims)	Total (For Society as a Whole)
Measured effect			
Child care	$ 683	$ 0	$ 683
K–12 education	0	3,297	3,297
Adult education	0	95	95
College[b]	0	-285	-285
Earnings[c]	2,802	1,154	3,955
Crime	0	13,774	13,774
Welfare	-657	723	66
Total measured	$2,828	$18,758	$21,585
Projected effect			
Earnings	1,074	442	1,517
Crime	0	2,046	2,046
Welfare	-66	73	7
Total projected	$1,008	$ 2,561	$ 3,570
Total measured & projected	$3,836	$21,319	$25,155
Cost of preschool program	0	-11,257	-11,257
Net benefit	$3,836	$10,062	$13,898

[a]Costs appear as negative numbers; benefits appear as positive numbers.

[b]Some small portion of college costs is likely to have been borne by the participants, but this could not be estimated from the available information.

[c]The benefits reported under *earnings* include all costs paid by the employer to hire a program participant. Allocation between participants and taxpayers assumes that the marginal tax rate is 25%, that the value of fringe benefits to the employee equals 10% of salary, and that other costs to the employer equal 10% of salary.

expected to be quite as impervious to drastic reductions as they are at lower discount rates, but the outcome remains remarkably robust with respect to downward revisions of estimated benefits. With the exception of crime, none of the benefit estimates is essential to obtaining a positive net benefit. In the case of crime, the value of estimated benefits to victims can be zero, and yet present value of the estimated net benefit remains positive. At least some portion of the estimated benefits from reductions in criminal justice system costs are required for the preschool program to pass the benefit-cost test. However, no *projected benefits* (beyond age 27) are required to conclude that the program was a sound investment. With a discount rate of 11%, each dollar of benefits after age 28 has a present value of less than 7 cents, and total projected benefits account for only about 10% of the present value of all estimated benefits. Finally, all benefit estimates and projections could be reduced by nearly half (47%), and estimated net present value would

Table 35

PRESCHOOL PROGRAM'S ESTIMATED EFFECTS PER PROGRAM PARTICIPANT
(PRESENT VALUE, 1992 DOLLARS DISCOUNTED AT 11%)

Effect[a]	For Participant Only	For General Public (Taxpayers/ Crime Victims)	Total (For Society as a Whole)
Measured effect			
Child care	$ 675	$ 0	$ 675
K–12 education	0	3,011	3,011
Adult education	0	80	80
College[b]	0	-240	-240
Earnings[c]	2,329	959	3,288
Crime	0	11,651	11,651
Welfare	-558	614	56
Total measured	**$2,446**	**$16,075**	**$18,521**
Projected effect			
Earnings	588	242	831
Crime	0	1,608	1,608
Welfare	-51	56	5
Total projected	**$ 537**	**$ 1,906**	**$ 2,444**
Total measured & projected	$2,983	$17,981	$20,965
Cost of preschool program	0	-11,114	-11,114
Net benefit	$2,983	$ 6,867	$ 9,851

[a]Costs appear as negative numbers; benefits appear as positive numbers.

[b]Some small portion of college costs is likely to have been borne by the participants, but this could not be estimated from the available information.

[c]The benefits reported under *earnings* include all costs paid by the employer to hire a program participant. Allocation between participants and taxpayers assumes that the marginal tax rate is 25%, that the value of fringe benefits to the employee equals 10% of salary, and that other costs to the employer equal 10% of salary.

remain positive. In other words, even if the true benefits were only about half of the estimated values, the High/Scope Perry Preschool program would still be a sound investment when discounted at the extraordinarily high rate of 11%.

Global Effects

A limitation of a controlled study in which an intervention is provided to only a small part of the target population is that it does not allow for the direct estimation of global effects. These are effects that occur as the result of the program group's effects on the environment. In this instance, the number of children attending the preschool program was so small that it is unlikely that they had a perceptible impact on their school and community. However, the more fundamental problem is that even if measurable global effects *were* produced in the High/Scope Perry Preschool Project, the experimental design offers no way to measure them.

Several types of positive global effects seem plausible. For example, if the preschool program were provided to *all* children in a given area, improvements in school performance might be so widespread as to change school climate, peer norms, teacher expectations, and even the level of instruction in the classroom. These effects would increase the school success of all children, increasing the effects of the program on those who attended and producing effects on those who did not attend. Similarly, decreases in teen pregnancy, delinquency, dropout rates, or welfare dependency all might create "bandwagon" effects due to changes in peer-group norms about acceptable behavior, and this could contribute to further reductions in these behaviors.

If all or most of the global effects from preschool education are positive, estimates from the High/Scope Perry Preschool analysis will underestimate program benefits. However, there is one type of global effect that tends to be negative and may bias results toward overestimation. In the case of two benefits — the reduction in education costs and the increases in earnings — there is potential for "queuing bias," which would occur if benefits for the program group were obtained by bumping others out of the queue for these benefits (not necessarily bumping no-program group members, because most of the population is outside the experiment). If the school district placed a fixed percentage of children in special education, replacing program group children with others who were next in line for special education, then there might have been no reduction in special education costs at all. Likewise, if increases in the employment of the program group led to decreases in the employment of others, there might have been less or even no net increase in earnings for the community as a whole. This would be the case if there were only a fixed number of jobs and only the most qualified (e.g., the top 90%) received jobs.

Whether or not queuing bias is a serious problem for this analysis is fundamentally a question about how schools and labor markets operate and, as such, it cannot be answered with the data at hand. Schools vary greatly in the percentage of students that they place in special education, and those with more proficient students tend to place smaller percentages than those with less proficient students. With respect to the labor market, the long-run demand for better educated labor seems quite elastic, and education seems to decrease the probability of unemployment in ways that suggest the queuing model of employment is substantially incorrect (Mincer, 1989; Murphy & Welch, 1989). Ultimately, investments in education may play a critical role in increasing productivity for the economy as a whole through resultant contributions to invention and innovation (Grossman & Helpman, 1994; Mincer, 1989).

In summary, the evidence indicates that both schools and labor markets are flexible enough to make queuing bias at most a minor problem — one that might be more than offset by unmeasured bandwagon effects. Moreover, even if the queuing bias were large relative to the estimated school cost and earnings benefits, the potential impact on the results would be well within the margin of error that can be accommodated without a change in the conclusions. Finally, if these global effects were so large that national investments in preschool education would fail to produce reductions in school costs and increases in earnings, it would be indicative of serious problems in education and national economic policy — problems requiring major policy reforms regardless of preschool education policy. Clearly such reforms are easier to propose than to implement. Fortunately, the sensitivity analyses demonstrate that even under the less favorable assumptions, such policy reforms would not be necessary for preschool education to be a sound investment.

Generalizing From This Benefit-Cost Analysis

Interest in the benefit-cost analysis of the High/Scope Perry Preschool program primarily stems from its potential implications for local, state, and national policy. The important question is whether providing publicly funded preschool programs for all economically disadvantaged children throughout the nation would yield a similar return. This question is addressed in Chapter 5 by considering (1) evidence from other studies of the effects of preschool programs and (2) the characteristics of preschool programs and children's lives today.

V Public Policy Implications

By any reasonable standard, the High/Scope Perry Preschool Program was a remarkable economic investment. The evidence for this is pictorially displayed in Figure 2 on the next page, which summarizes the results of this benefit-cost analysis using a real discount rate of 3%. The preschool program succeeded in its primary goal of improving the lives of the children who attended the program, both financially and in ways that could not be measured in dollars. Beyond anyone's expectations, it also succeeded in its secondary goal of producing social and economic benefits for the taxpayers who financed the preschool program. The indirect benefits to the taxpayers and the rest of society generally (in the terminology of economics, the *externalities*) far exceeded both the costs and the direct benefits.

Against the initial cost per child of $12,356, the total measured benefits to society as a whole are estimated at $242,646 per child undiscounted, which is $108,002 per child discounted at 3% and $43,856 per child discounted at 7%. Using the most reasonable of these discount rates, 3%, we can conclude that the High/Scope Perry Preschool program returned to society as a whole $8.74 per dollar invested — which is a benefit-cost ratio of nearly 9 to 1. This $8.74 includes $7.16 in benefits to the general public (taxpayers and crime victims) and $1.58 in benefits to program participants. Moreover, the conclusion that the program was an economic winner holds up under a wide range of alternative assumptions.

To put these figures in perspective, the economic return from the High/Scope Perry Preschool program was so extraordinary that the program outperformed the stock market over the same period. From January 1963 to December 1993, a capitalization-weighted index of stocks traded on the New York Stock Exchange (NYSE), the American Stock Exchange (ASE), and the National Association of Securities Dealers Automated Quotation (NASDAQ) system produced an average annual return of 11.83% (Seyhun, 1994). Over the same period, inflation averaged just over 5% as measured by the Consumer Price Index and the GDP implicit price deflator (U.S. Bureau of the Census, 1995), meaning that the real return on the stock market during that period was about 6.8%. By comparison, the High/Scope Perry Preschool program produced a real (i.e., inflation-adjusted) annual rate of return that exceeded 11 percent. Thus, the return on preschool education surpassed by a comfortable margin the average return on stocks, which is far higher than the return on less risky investments such as government securities.

Research Supporting High/Scope Perry Preschool Project Findings

This economic analysis is based on a single preschool program, but the High/Scope Perry Preschool program is not an extreme example. Over the past 30 years many other preschool programs — including Head Start and public school preschool programs — have produced the same types of positive effects on schooling and achievement as did the High/Scope Perry Preschool program (Barnett, 1995; Schweinhart et al., 1993). This support

Figure 2
COSTS AND BENEFITS FOR SOCIETY
PER PRESCHOOL PROGRAM PARTICIPANT

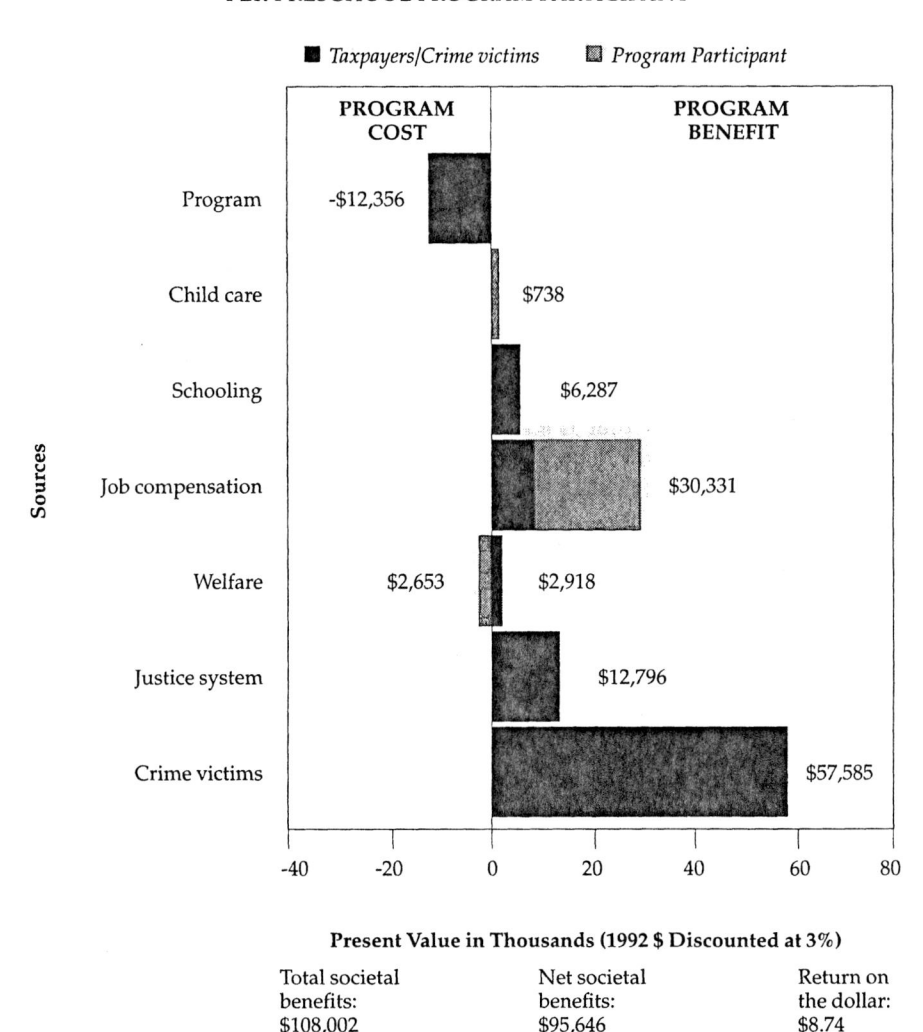

■ Taxpayers/Crime victims   ▒ Program Participant

Sources	PROGRAM COST	PROGRAM BENEFIT
Program	-$12,356	
Child care		$738
Schooling		$6,287
Job compensation		$30,331
Welfare	$2,653	$2,918
Justice system		$12,796
Crime victims		$57,585

Present Value in Thousands (1992 $ Discounted at 3%)

Total societal benefits: $108,002   Net societal benefits: $95,646   Return on the dollar: $8.74

Note: From Significant Benefits (p.167), by L. J. Schweinhart et al., 1993, Ypsilanti, MI: High/Scope Press. Copyright 1993 by High/Scope Educational Research Foundation.

is broadened by research in economics that firmly links educational success to the other relevant outcomes: earnings and employment, welfare dependency, crime, and family formation and fertility patterns (Ashenfelter & Krueger, 1994; Becker, 1975, 1981; Cohn & Geske, 1990; Freeman 1996; Haveman & Wolfe, 1984, 1995; Maynard, 1995; Witte, 1994). Thus, if the educational results can be produced, the other results and the economic return should follow.

Many studies, including several Head Start studies, have found effects larger than those found in the High/Scope Perry Preschool study. Significant reduction in grade repetition, in particular, is a common finding, although the reduction in grade repetition was not found to be statistically significant in the High/Scope Perry Preschool study. For example, Monroe and McDonald (1981) found that a Head Start program in Rome, Georgia, reduced grade repetition by 12 percentage points in addition to reducing special education placements by 14 percentage points and increasing high school graduation by 17 percentage points. In a national study, Barnett and Camilli (1996) found evidence that Head Start substantially reduces the frequency of grade repetition. Looking at results across more than 20 longitudinal studies reveals that the larger reductions in grade repetition were produced in areas having higher overall rates of grade repetition (Barnett, 1995). School district policies in Ypsilanti, Michigan, and surrounding communities appear to have minimized grade repetition, thereby limiting the potential for the High/Scope program to reduce it.

The Potential of Preschool Programs Today

Of course, no one should expect that today, preschool education programs will produce for every child in every community exactly the same long-term economic benefits as were found in the longitudinal High/Scope Perry Preschool study. As an ecological approach to human development such as Bronfenbrenner's (1991) person-process-context model suggests, the results are likely to vary with

- The children and families served
- The quality and quantity of preschool care and education provided
- The broader environments in which children live

The Population Served

The children and families served by the High/Scope Perry Preschool program were all poor and African-American. Clearly they were at high risk for the difficulties that preschool helped them to at least partially overcome or avoid: school failure, crime and delinquency, unemployment and low income, teenage pregnancy and single-parenting. Poor children from all ethnic groups have increased risks for these difficulties, and studies that have looked for outcome differences across ethnic groups find no evidence that children from other ethnic groups benefit any less from preschool programs than do African-American children (Barnett, 1995) Although risks to children decrease as income rises (thereby reducing potential benefits from preschool programs), these risks do not suddenly disappear when family income crosses the poverty line. Given the large margin by which benefits exceed costs in the High/Scope Perry Preschool study, many children in families above the poverty line might benefit enough to justify the costs of providing widespread public preschool programs.

Program Quality

In some respects, the High/Scope Perry Preschool program was of higher quality than many of today's preschool programs. Being relatively well financed even by today's standards, it could hire a highly qualified teacher for every 6 or 7 children served. This compares with staffing ratios of 7.4 children per adult in public school programs, 8.4 children per adult in Head Start programs, and 8.4 to 11.0 children per adult in private child care centers, where many of the adults are less qualified teachers or teacher aides (Willer et al., 1991). In the High/Scope Perry Preschool program, given the teachers' superior qualifications, the close supervision, and the favorable child/adult ratio, it seems likely that children's classroom experiences were of relatively high quality. Today, per child costs for a program of similar quality would be $7,000 to $8,000 per year. By contrast, even after recent increases in funding to support increased quality, Head Start's average federal expenditure was only $4,334 per child in 1994 (Robinson, 1995).

Program Quantity

Today's public preschool programs for disadvantaged children primarily serve children for a single year at age 4, whereas the High/Scope Perry Preschool program served most children for 2 years, beginning at age 3. However, the High/Scope study's sample size did not permit examination of differences in effects between 1 and 2 years of service, and other studies do not provide much more information on this matter. Cross-study comparisons provided some evidence that beginning preschool education earlier and continuing it longer produces larger effects (Barnett, 1995; Campbell & Ramey, 1995). At present, the best estimate is that there are diminishing marginal returns — as the duration of preschool education increases, the beneficial effects increase, but less than proportionately. This implies that 1 year of preschool education is a good investment, but that 2 or more might be even better. Future research clarifying the additional payoff of earlier and lengthier preschool education programs would be extremely valuable for policymakers.

However, it should be recognized that not all of the "quantity" advantages are on one side (Zigler & Styfco, 1994). Not only High/Scope but others have continued to develop curricula that address both enduring and changing needs of children and society. Compared with the High/Scope Perry Preschool program, programs like Head Start provide a much more comprehensive *set* of services, and many of today's child care programs operate for a greater portion of the year. Head Start provides access to preventive health and mental health services, dental care, nutrition, a wide range of parent involvement activities, and family support services (Zigler & Styfco, 1994). Clearly, there is room for increased support of quality in existing programs; at the same time, it would be a mistake if those seeking to replicate the High/Scope Perry Preschool program's results were to throw out the comprehensive services or expanded hours that some public programs now offer.

The Broader Environment

Children today grow up in a world that is different from the one experienced by the children in the High/Scope Perry Preschool program. Some of the problems that children and society face have worsened, whereas others have improved. The following changes, together with recent changes in public policy, are likely to affect children and the potential benefits from preschool programs:

- Despite continuing funding inequalities across and within school systems, expenditures in the schools attended by poor children have risen, and the test scores of these children have risen as well (Witte, 1994).
- Special education is more common than ever, and grade repetition, though there are no reliable national figures on it, seems high.
- Crime seems to be going down generally, but violent crime by children is increasing.
- More than ever, education is seen as a critical factor for earning a decent living.
- Welfare assistance programs are being reformed, but whether the reforms are an improvement for young children remains to be seen.

Overall, in light of these changes, it seems likely that high-quality preschool education will continue to have positive effects with economic benefits that are large, perhaps even larger in the future than they have been in the past.

The most important difference between the future and the past may be that **the overwhelming majority of children will experience nonparental early care and education as maternal employment becomes nearly universal, especially among poor mothers in poverty.** This raises the possibility of reaping much larger economic benefits from full-day preschool programs that enable mothers to work — reducing mothers' time out of the labor force increases not only their current but also their future earnings. As full-day preschool programs become more common, the child development issue will of course shift from comparing the effects of home care with those of a high-quality preschool program to comparing the effects of mediocre or even low-quality programs with those of high-quality programs.

The Need for Further Research

There is great need for experimental research evaluating the economic returns produced by increasing the quality and quantity of early care and education. In the early childhood field, no research is more important than conducting longitudinal randomized trials to study the benefits of high-quality early care and education for children and their parents. We would do well to model at least some of these trials on the longitudinal High/Scope Perry Preschool study, which was relatively small in size, had minimal attrition, and emphasized collecting a great deal of high-quality data.

In sum, when the economic analysis of the High/Scope Perry Preschool program is placed in the context of the larger research literature, the evidence supports generalizing its basic results to current public programs. The need for further research should not prevent society from acting on what is already known. A conservative approach would be to provide Head Start and public school preschool programs with the resources required to deliver high-quality services to all poor children and to gradually expand services in pilot projects to investigate the benefits of offering full-day care to young children in near-poor families.

Ignoring the Evidence — What Are the Costs?

The Clinton Administration has proposed to make Head Start available to every poor child by 1999. At this writing, that promise has been undermined by Congress, which has proposed to cut Head Start funding for 1996 (Children's Defense Fund, 1996) and has so far failed to fund Head Start at the levels required to meet the Administration's goal. At present, Head Start serves only about a third of the eligible population, and state and local programs make up only a small fraction of the difference (Robinson, 1995).

This failure to provide early childhood programs to all poor children costs taxpayers an enormous amount. If just half of all poor children in the United States go unserved, the lost benefits to society from our failure to provide high-quality preschool programs amount to $50 billion dollars annually (based on the High/Scope Perry Preschool program benefits discounted at a 3% annual rate). Moreover, if half of potential program benefits are lost because current programs are not of sufficiently high quality, an additional $25 billion dollars are lost annually. By contrast, the annual cost of extending the current Head Start program to all poor children for 1 year would be only $2.5 billion. Even raising spending to $8,000 per year for high-quality programs for 2 years for the approximately 2 million poor 3- and 4-year-olds in the U.S. would cost only $12 billion (in addition to current Head Start spending), against a potential $75 billion in added benefits.

Clearly, the *economic* costs of failing to act on the evidence about preschool education are vast, but we should not forget that **behind the cost and benefit figures are the lives of real people.** Their lives, and our lives, hang in the balance. Latest estimates place the victim costs of crime at $451 billion per year, roughly $1,800 for every person in the country (Oliver, 1996). In 1993, 10% of men 25 to 34 years old were incarcerated, on probation, or on parole, and 34% of African-American male high school dropouts in this age-range were incarcerated (Freeman, 1996). Teen pregnancy is rising, and 31% of all births in 1993 were to unmarried mothers (Children's Defense Fund, 1996). The gap between rich and poor is growing, and the poor are becoming poorer (Children's Defense Fund, 1996). High-quality preschool education is not a panacea, but it can lead to meaningful improvement in all these aspects of life. In his 1961 Inaugural Address, President Kennedy said, "If a free society cannot help the many who are poor, it cannot save the few who are rich." This economic analysis shows just how right he was.

Appendix

Table A1

CORRELATIONS BETWEEN PROGRAM OUTCOMES AND
MOTHER EMPLOYED AT STUDY ENTRY

Variable	Full Sample[a]	Males[b]	Females[c]
Educational attainment at age 27	.168*	.230*	.096
High school graduation	.056	.214*	-.148
Years of educable mental impairment classes	-.202**	-.252**	-.147
Arrests	-.041	-.039	-.140
Adult arrests	-.130	-.097	-.160
Months on welfare in past 10 years	.000	-.153	.020
Months on welfare in past 5 years	.026	-.129	.072
Ever on welfare	-.021	-.037	-.019
Annual earnings at age 27	.078	.192	-.052
Monthly earnings at age 27	.064	.140	-.033

[a]$N = 115$ to 123 [b]$N = 66$ to 72 [c]$N = 46$ to 51

*$p > .05$ but $< .10$ **$p < .05$

References

Adams, G., & Sandfort, J. (1994). *First steps, promising futures*. Washington, DC: Children's Defense Fund.

Anderson, E. (1990). *Streetwise: Race, class, and change in an urban community*. Chicago: University of Chicago Press.

Ashenfelter, O., & Krueger, A. (1994). Estimates of the economic return to schooling from a new sample of twins. *American Economic Review, 84*, 1157–1194.

Barnett, W. S. (1985a). Benefit-cost analysis of the Perry Preschool program and its policy implications. *Educational Evaluation and Policy Analysis, 7*(4), 333–342.

Barnett, W. S. (1985b). *The Perry Preschool program and its long-term effects: A benefit-cost analysis*. (High/Scope Policy Papers, No. 2.). Ypsilanti, MI: High/Scope Press.

Barnett, W. S. (1992). Benefits of compensatory preschool education. *Journal of Human Resources, 27*(2), 279–312.

Barnett, W. S. (1993a). Benefit-cost analysis of preschool education: Findings from a 25-year follow-up. *American Journal of Orthopsychiatry, 63*(4), 500–508.

Barnett, W. S. (1993b). Cost-benefit analysis. In L. J. Schweinhart, H. V. Barnes, & D. P. Weikart (with W. S. Barnett & A. Epstein), *Significant benefits: The High/Scope Perry Preschool study through age 27* (Monographs of the High/Scope Educational Research Foundation, 10; pp. 142–192). Ypsilanti, MI: High/Scope Press.

Barnett, W. S. (1995). Long-term effects of early childhood programs on cognitive and school outcomes. *The Future of Children, 5*(3), 25–50.

Barnett, W. S., & Camilli, G. (1996). *Definite results from loose data: A response to "Does Head Start Make a Difference?"*. New Brunswick, NJ: Rutgers University, Graduate School of Education.

Barnett, W. S., & Escobar, C. M. (1987). The economics of early intervention. A review. *Review of Educational Research, 57*(4), 387–414.

Barnett, W. S., & Escobar, C. M. (1990). Economic costs and benefits of early intervention. In S. J. Meisels & J. P. Shonkoff (Eds.), *Handbook of early intervention: Theory, practice and analysis* (pp. 560–582). Cambridge, MA: Cambridge University Press.

Baumeister, A., Kupstas, F., & Klindworth, L. (1991). The new morbidity. *American Behavioral Scientist, 34*(4), 468–500.

Becker, G. (1975). *Human capital* (2nd ed.). New York: Columbia University Press.

Becker, G. (1981). *A treatise on the family*. Cambridge, MA: Harvard University Press.

Berrueta-Clement, J. R., Schweinhart, L. J., Barnett, W. S., Epstein, A. S., & Weikart, D. P. (1984). *Changed lives: The effects of the Perry Preschool program on youths through age 19* (Monographs of the High/Scope Educational Research Foundation, 8). Ypsilanti, MI: High/Scope Press.

Bronfenbrenner, U. (1991). *An ecological paradigm for research on child care*. Unpublished manuscript, Cornell University, Department of Human Development and Family Studies, Ithaca, NY.

Bruner, J. (1980). *Under five in Britain*. Ypsilanti, MI: High/Scope Press.

Campbell, F. A., & Ramey, C. T. (1995, Winter). Cognitive and school outcomes for high-risk African-American students at middle adolescence: Positive effects of early intervention. *American Educational Research Journal, 32*, 743–772.

Children's Defense Fund. (1996). *The state of America's children, Yearbook 1996*. Washington, DC: Children's Defense Fund.

Cohen, M. A. (1988). Pain, suffering, and jury awards: A study of the cost of crime to victims. *Law & Society Review, 22*(3), 537–555.

Cohen, M. A. (1990). A note on the cost of crime to victims. *Urban Studies, 27*(1), 139–146.

Cohn, E., & Geske, T. G. (1990). *The economics of education* (3rd ed.). Oxford: Pergamon Press.

Committee on Ways and Means (Staff), U.S. House of Representatives. (1991). *1991 Greenbook: Background material and data on programs within the jurisdiction of the Committee on Ways and Means* (102d Cong., 1st Sess.). Washington, DC: U.S. Government Printing Office.

Daniel, J., Hampton, R., & Newberger, E. (1983). Child abuse and accidents in Black families: A controlled comparative study. *American Journal of Orthopsychiatry, 53*(4), 645–653.

Datcher-Loury, L. (1989). Family background and school achievement among low-income Blacks. *Journal of Human Resources, 24*(3), 528–544.

Duncan, G. J. (1976). Earnings functions and nonpecuniary benefits. *Journal of Human Resources, 9*(4), 462–483.

Duncan, G. J. (1988). Special tabulations of the Panel Study of Income Dynamics. In Committee on Ways and Means (Staff), U.S. House of Representatives, *1992 Greenbook: Background material and data on programs within the jurisdiction of the Committee on Ways and Means* (102d Cong., 2d Sess.). Washington, DC: U.S. Government Printing Office.

Duncan, G. J., Hill, M. S., & Hoffman, S. D. (1988). Welfare dependence within and across generations. *Science, 239,* 467–471.

Ellwood, D. (1986). *Targeting the would-be long-term recipient of AFDC: Who should be served?* Princeton, NJ: Mathematica.

Federal Bureau of Investigation. (1980). *Crime in America* (Uniform Crime Reports). Washington, DC: U.S. Government Printing Office.

Federal Bureau of Investigation. (1991). *Crime in America* (Uniform Crime Reports). Washington, DC: U.S. Government Printing Office.

Federal Bureau of Investigation. (1992a). *Crime in America* (Uniform Crime Reports). Washington, DC: U.S. Government Printing Office.

Federal Bureau of Investigation. (1992b). *Crime in the United States, 1990.* Rockville, MD: Justice Statistics Clearinghouse, U.S. Department of Justice.

Freeman, R. B. (1996). Why do so many young American men commit crimes and what might we do about it? *Journal of Economic Perspectives, 10*(1), 25–42.

Fullerton, D., & Rogers, D. L. (1993). *Who bears the lifetime tax burden.* Washington, DC: Brookings Institution.

Gottschalk, P. (1992). The intergenerational transmission of welfare participation: Facts and possible causes. *Journal of Policy Analysis and Management, 11*(2), 254–272.

Gramlich, E. (1981). *Benefit-cost analysis of government programs.* Englewood Cliffs, NJ: Prentice-Hall.

Gross, M. L. (1992). *The government racket: Washington waste from A to Z.* New York: Bantam.

Grossman, G. M., & Helpman, E. (1994). Endogenous innovation in the theory of growth. *Journal of Economic Perspectives, 8*(1), 23–44.

Guralnik, J., Land, K., Blazer, D., Fillenbaum, G., & Branch, L. (1993). Educational status and active life expectancy among older Blacks and Whites. *New England Journal of Medicine, 329*(2), 110–116.

Hack, M., Breslau, N., Weissman, B., Aram, D., Klein, N., & Borawski, E. (1991). Effect of very low birth weight and subnormal head size on cognitive abilities at school age. *New England Journal of Medicine, 325,* 231–237.

Haveman, R. H., & Wolfe, B. L. (1984). Schooling and economic well-being: The role of non-market effects. *Journal of Human Resources, 19*(3), 377–407.

Haveman, R. H., & Wolfe, B. L. (1995). The determinants of children's attainments: A review of methods and findings. *Journal of Economic Literature, 33,* 1829–1878.

Hill, C. R. (1981). Education and earnings: A review of the evidence. *Economics of Education Review, 1*(4), 403–420.

Hofferth, S. L., West, J., Henke, R., & Kaufman, P. (1994). *Access to early childhood programs for children at risk.* Washington, DC: National Center for Education Statistics.

Howes, C., Phillips, D. A., & Whitebook, M. (1992). Thresholds of quality: Implications for the social development of children in center-based child care. *Child Development, 63,* 449–460.

Jargowsky, P. A., & Bane, M. J. (1991). Ghetto poverty in the United States, 1970–1980. In C. Jencks & P.E. Peterson (Eds.), *The urban underclass* (pp. 274–298). Washington, DC: Brookings Institution.

Jencks, C. (1991). Is the American underclass growing? In C. Jencks & P.E. Peterson (Eds.), *The urban underclass* (pp. 28–102). Washington, DC: Brookings Institution.

Jencks, C., & Edin, K. (1990). The real welfare problem. *American Prospect, 1*(2), 31–50.

Jorgenson, D., & Fraumeni, B. (1989). Investment in education. *Educational Researcher, 18*(4), 35–44.

Just, R. E, Hueth, D. L, & Schmitz, A. (1982). *Applied welfare economics and public policy.* Englewood Cliffs, NJ: Prentice-Hall.

Kolb, J., & Scheraga, J. (1990). Discounting the benefits and costs of environmental regulations. *Journal of Policy Analysis and Management, 9*(3), 381–390.

Kuh, D., & Wadsworth, M. (1991). Childhood influences on adult male earnings in a longitudinal study. *British Journal of Sociology, 42*(4), 537–555.

Lemieux, T., Fortin, B., & Frechette, P. (1994). The effect of taxes on labor supply in the underground economy. *American Economic Review, 84*(1), 231–254.

Levy, F., & Murnane, R. J. (1992). U.S. earnings levels and earnings inequality: A review of recent trends and proposed explanations. *Journal of Economic Literature, 30*, 1333–1381.

Lind, R. (1982). A primer on the major issues relating to the discount rate for evaluating national energy options. In R. Lind, K. Arrow, G. Corey, P. Dasgupta, A. Sen, T. Stauffer, J. Stiglitz, J. Stockfisch, & R. Wilson, *Discounting for time and risk in energy policy* (pp. 21–94). Washington, DC: Resources for the Future and Johns Hopkins University Press.

Low, S., & Spindler, P. (1968). *Child care arrangements of working mothers in the United States.* Washington, DC: U.S. Department of Health, Education and Welfare, Children's Bureau, and U.S. Department of Labor, Women's Bureau.

Mathios, A. D. (1988). Education, variation in earnings, and nonmonetary compensation. *Journal of Human Resources, 24*(3), 456–468.

Maynard, R. A. (1995, January). *The social benefits of education: Family structure, fertility, and child welfare.* Paper presented at a conference, sponsored by the U.S. Department of Education, on The Social Benefits of Education: Can They Be Measured?, Arlie, VA.

Mikesell, R. (1977). *The rate of discount for evaluating public projects.* Washington, DC: American Enterprise Institute.

Miller, H. P., & Hornseth, R. A. (1967). *Present value of estimated lifetime earnings* (Technical Paper No. 16). Washington, DC: U.S. Department of Commerce, Bureau of the Census.

Milne, A., Myers, D., Rosenthal, A., & Ginsburg, A. (1986). Single parents, working mothers, and the educational achievement of school children. *Sociology of Education, 59*, 125–139.

Mincer, J. (1974). *Schooling, experience and earnings.* New York: National Bureau of Economic Research and Columbia University.

Mincer, J. (1989). Human capital and the labor market: A review of current research. *Educational Researcher, 18*(4), 27–34.

Mitchell, A., Seligson, M., & Marx, F. (1989). *Early childhood programs and the public schools: Between promise and practice.* Dover, MA: Auburn House.

Mishan, E. J. (1976). *Cost-benefit analysis.* New York: Praeger.

Monroe, E., & McDonald, M. S. (1981). *Follow-up study of the 1966 Head Start program, Rome City Schools, Rome, Georgia.* Unpublished paper.

Moore, M. T., Strang, E. W., Schwartz, M., & Braddock, M. (1988). *Patterns in special education service delivery and cost* (Report prepared for the U.S. Department of Education). Washington, DC: Decision Resources Corporation.

Murphy, K., & Welch, F. (1989). Wage premiums for college graduates: Recent growth and possible explanations. *Educational Researcher, 18*(4), 17–26.

National Center for Education Statistics. (1992). *Current funds revenues and expenditures of institutions of higher education: Fiscal years 1982–1990.* Washington, DC: Author.

National Center for Education Statistics. (1993). *Condition of education, 1992.* Washington, DC: U.S. Government Printing Office.

National Center for Health Statistics. (1993). *U.S. 1989 abridged life tables*. Hyattsville, MD: Author, Public Health Service, U.S. Department of Health and Human Services.

Oliver, C. (1996, May 20). Costs of crime and punishment. *Investor's Business Daily*, pp. 1–2.

Olsen, R. J. (1994). Fertility and the size of the U.S. labor force. *Journal of Economic Literature, 32*(1), 60–100.

Pappas, G., Queen, S., Hadden, W., & Fisher, G. (1993). The increasing disparity in mortality between socioeconomic groups in the United States, 1960 and 1986. *New England Journal of Medicine, 329*(2), 103–109.

Pechman, J. A. (1985). *Who paid the taxes, 1966–1985?* Washington, DC: Brookings Institution.

Research and Policy Committee of the Committee for Economic Development. (1985). *Investing in our children: Business and the public schools*. New York: Committee for Economic Development.

Research and Policy Committee of the Committee for Economic Development. (1987). *Children in need: Investment strategies for the educationally disadvantaged*. New York: Committee for Economic Development.

Robinson, D. H. (1995). *Head Start in the 104th Congress* (CRS Report for Congress, 95-431 EPW, updated March 29). Washington, DC: Library of Congress, Congressional Research Service.

Rodes, T. W. (1975). *National child care consumer study: 1975. Volume II: Current patterns of child care use in the United States* (Report by Unco, Inc.). Washington, DC: U.S. Department of Heath, Education and Welfare, Office of Child Development.

Rodes, T. W., & Moore, J. C., (1975). *National child care consumer study. Volume I: Basic tabulations* (Report by Unco, Inc.). Washington, DC: U.S. Department of Heath, Education and Welfare, Office of Child Development.

Ruopp, R., Travers, J., Glantz, F., & Coelen, C. (1979). *Children at the center: Final report of the National Day Care Study*. Cambridge, MA: Abt Associates.

Schultz, T. (1971). *Investments in human capital: The role of education and research*. New York: Macmillan.

Schweinhart, L. J., Barnes, H. V., & Weikart, D.P. (with Barnett, W. S., & Epstein, A. S.). (1993). *Significant benefits: The High/Scope Perry Preschool study through age 27* (Monographs of the High/Scope Educational Research Foundation, 10). Ypsilanti, MI: High/Scope Press.

Schweinhart, L. J., & Weikart, D. P. (1980). *Young children grow up: The effects of the Perry Preschool program on youths through age 15* (Monographs of the High/Scope Educational Research Foundation, 7). Ypsilanti, MI: High/Scope Press.

Seitz, V., & Apfel, N. (1994). Effects of family support intervention: Diffusion effects to siblings. *Child Development, 65*, 677–683.

Seyhun, H. N. (1994). *Stock market extremes and portfolio performance*. New York, NY: Towneley Capital Management.

Stevens, A. H. (1994). The dynamics of poverty spells: Updating Bane and Elwood. *American Economic Review, 84*(2), 34–37.

Stockfisch, J. A. (1982). Measuring the social rate of return on private investment. In R. Lind, K. Arrow, G. Corey, P. Dasgupta, A. Sen, T. Stauffer, J. Stiglitz, J. Stockfisch, & R. Wilson, *Discounting for time and risk in energy policy* (pp. 257–272). Washington, DC: Resources for the Future and Johns Hopkins University Press.

Terman, L. M., & Merrill, M. A. (1960). *Stanford-Binet Intelligence Scale Form L–M: Manual for the third revision*. Boston, MA: Houghton Mifflin.

Thompson, M. S. (1980). *Benefit-cost analysis for program evaluation*. Beverly Hills: Sage.

U.S. Administration on Children, Youth and Families. (1995). *Project Head Start statistical fact sheet*. Washington, DC: U.S. Government Printing Office.

U.S. Bureau of the Census. (1982). *Trends in child care arrangements of working mothers* (Current Population Reports, Series P-23, No. 117). Washington, DC: U.S. Government Printing Office.

U.S. Bureau of the Census. (1983). *Lifetime earnings estimates for men and women in the United States: 1979* (Current Population Reports, Series P-60, No. 139). Washington, DC: U.S. Government Printing Office.

U.S. Bureau of the Census. (1992a). *Money income of households, families, and persons in the United States: 1991* (Current Population Reports, Series P-60, No. 180). Washington, DC: U.S. Government Printing Office.

U.S. Bureau of the Census. (1992b). *Statistical abstract of the United States: 1992.* Washington, DC: U.S. Government Printing Office.

U.S. Bureau of the Census. (1995). *Statistical abstract of the United States: 1995.* Washington, DC: U.S. Government Printing Office.

U.S. Bureau of Economic Analysis. (1993). *Survey of current business.* Washington, DC: Author, U.S. Department of Commerce.

U.S. Bureau of Justice Statistics. (1992). *Criminal victimization in the United States, 1990.* Rockville, MD: Justice Statistics Clearinghouse, U.S. Department of Justice.

U.S. Bureau of Labor Statistics. (1992, June). *Employer costs for employee compensation — March 1992.* (U.S. Department of Labor NEWS, No. 92–391). Washington, DC: Author, U.S. Department of Labor.

U.S. General Accounting Office. (1990). *Early childhood education: What are the costs of high-quality programs?* (GAO/HRD-90-43BR). Gaithersburg, MD: Author.

U.S. General Accounting Office. (1992). *Early intervention: Federal investments like WIC can produce savings* (GAO/HRD-92-18). Gaithersburg, MD: Author.

Varden, S. A. (1982). Public school systems. In R. E. Anderson & E. S. Kasl (Eds.), *The costs and financing of adult education and training* (pp. 33–56). Lexington, MA: Lexington Books.

Weber, C. U., Foster, P. W., & Weikart, D. P. (1978). *An economic analysis of the Ypsilanti Perry Preschool Project* (Monographs of the High/Scope Educational Research Foundation, 5). Ypsilanti, MI: High/Scope Press.

Weikart, D. P. (1967). *Preschool intervention: Preliminary results of the Perry Preschool Project.* Ann Arbor, MI: Campus Publishers.

Weikart, D. P., Bond, J. T., & McNeil, J. T. (1978). *The Ypsilanti Perry Preschool Project: Preschool years and longitudinal results through fourth grade* (Monographs of the High/Scope Educational Research Foundation, 3). Ypsilanti, MI: High/Scope Press.

Weikart, D. P., Deloria, D. J., Lawser, S. A., & Wiegerink, R. (1970; reprint 1993). *Longitudinal results of the Ypsilanti Perry Preschool Project* (Monographs of the High/Scope Educational Research Foundation, 1). Ypsilanti, MI: High/Scope Press.

Willer, B., Hofferth, S. L., Kisker, E. E., Divine-Hawkins, P., Farquhar, E., & Glantz, F. B. (1991). *The demand and supply of child care in 1990.* Washington, DC: National Association for the Education of Young Children.

Wilson, W. J. (1987). *The truly disadvantaged: The inner city, the underclass, and public policy.* Chicago: University of Chicago Press.

Witte, A. D. (1994, September). *Social benefits of education: Crime.* Paper presented at a conference, sponsored by the U.S. Department of Education, on The Social Benefits of Education: Can They Be Measured?, Arlie, VA.

Woodbury, S. A., & Hamermesh, D. S. (1992). Taxes, fringe benefits, and faculty. *Review of Economics and Statistics, 74*(2), 287–296.

Zedlewski, E. W. (1987, July). *Making confinement decisions.* (Research in Brief). Washington, DC: National Institute of Justice, U.S. Department of Justice.

Zigler, E., & Styfco, S. J. (1994). Is the Perry Preschool better than Head Start? Yes and no. *Early Childhood Research Quarterly, 9*(3, 4). 269–288.

Index

A

Administration on Children, Youth and Families, xii
Administrative costs, 8, 20–21, 22, 31
Adult secondary education, 13, 35–36
Aggregation, 13, 65 ff.
Aid to Families With Dependent Children (AFDC), 58, 59, 60, 61
American Stock Exchange, 85
Attrition, 4, 6, 45, 90

B

Bandwagon effects, 12, 82
Barnett, W. Steven, 87
Benefit categories, 13
Benefit-cost analysis, 85
    generalizing the results, 71
    methodology of, 3, 6–16
    and public policy, 7, 71, 83, 90
    underestimation of benefits, 70
Benefit-cost estimation assumptions, 72–74
    crime cost reduction, 73
    earnings, 73–74
    higher education, 38, 66
    productivity growth, 73–74
    welfare cost reduction, 73
Benefit-cost ratio, xi, 85
Benefits of High/Scope Perry Preschool program, 9–10
    assumptions about earnings, 66–67
    assumptions about higher education, 66–67
    categories of, 13
    crime reduction, 50
    distribution of, 13, 15, 65–68, 69, 70, 77–81
    economic value of, 12–15
    gender differences in, 68
    health, 75
    indirect, 12, 66, 67
    nonmonetary, 76, 77–78
    omitted, 74–76
    per program participant, 66, 69, 70, 77–81
    projected, 45, 55, 80
Bronfenbrenner, U., 87
Bush, George, xi

C

Camilli, G., 87
Capital costs, 8, 23, 31
Causal model, 11
Child care, 9, 89
    market value of program's, 27–28, 66, 69, 70, 77–81
Children, risks to, 87
Children's Defense Fund, 90
Clinton Administration, 90, xi
Cohen, M. A., 51–53
Committee for Economic Development, xi
Committee on Ways and Means, 1991, 60
Compensation, total. *See also* Earnings
    estimating the value of, 48
    program effects on, 49
Compensatory education, 30, 32, 33, 34
Congress, xii, 90
Consumer Price Index, 85
Correlation analysis, 71
Cost of High/Scope Perry Preschool program, 8–10, 85–86. *See also* Distribution of costs and benefits
    administrative and support staff, 20–21, 22
    calculation of, 19–27
    capital, 23
    developmental screening, 22–23
    and inflation, 24
    instructional staff, 20, 21
    lowering of, 26–27
    operating, 20, 22
    opportunity, 24
    to participants, 24
    per child, 20, 26, 85
    school district overhead, 20, 21, 22
    weighted-average estimate, 25–26, 35
Crime costs, 49–50
    and arrest rates, 51, 55
    beyond age 28, 55

correction costs, 54
estimated for preschool program participants, 56
gender differences in, 57, 68
justice system costs, 50, 51, 53, 54, 56, 57
reduction, 50, 56, 57
through age 28, 50–54
transfer payment costs, 53, 67
victim costs, 50, 51, 52, 53, 56, 57, 90
Crime effects, 11
Crime in the United States (Federal Bureau of Investigation), 51
Criminal Victimization in the United States (U.S. Bureau of Justice Statistics), 51
Current Population Survey, 44
Custodial care, 27

D

Depreciation, 23, 24, 25
Disciplinary education, 30, 32, 33, 34
Discount rate, 14–15, 65, 67, 69, 85
alternatives, 58, 65, 69, 76–77
and program benefits, 77–81
Distribution of costs and benefits, 13, 15, 65–68, 69, 70, 77–81
Dollar value, adjustment of, 13–15
Duncan, G. J., 60

E

Early childhood education, economic analysis of, 3, 88, 90
Earnings, 44, 49, 86. *See also* Compensation
benefits, 66–67
beyond age 27, 45–47
and education, 42, 43, 45
gender differences, 42, 68
no-program group, 41, 42–43
program group, 41, 42–43
projected lifetime, 45, 46, 47
through age 27, 41–44
Economic analysis, 3
Economic-value estimates, 77–78
Educational attainment, 42, 45, 86
Educational costs, elementary and secondary, 28
gender differences in, 34–35
per child, 33–35
placement categories for calculating, 30
procedure for calculating, 31–35
psychological evaluation, 30–32
Educational histories of study participants, 28, 42
Educational placement, elementary and secondary, 29
cost categories, 30, 34
Elementary and secondary education. *See* Educational costs, elementary and secondary
Ellwood, D., 60
Employment, 86
gender differences, 42–44, 46–47, 74
preschool program effect on, 11, 41 ff., 49
Environmental changes, 89
Externalities, 66, 67

F

Family configuration, 6
Federal Bureau of Investigation, 51, 55
Female labor force participation, 46, 74
Fixed capital, 23
distribution of, 24
Follow-up study, age-10, 4
Follow-up study, age-19, 4, 36, 41
Follow-up study, age-27, 4, 36, 41, 44, 46, 47
Food stamps, 58, 59, 60
Fringe benefits, 41, 48

G

GED preparation classes, 35
Gender differences, 6, 46–47, 68–70
in benefits, 68, 69
in crime cost savings, 68
in earnings, 42, 43, 46–47, 68, 74
and education costs, 34–35
in educational histories, 35, 37, 38, 42, 68, 74
in employment histories, 42, 74
in welfare costs, 61
General Accounting Office, 26
General Assistance (GA), 58, 59, 60
General education, 31, 33, 34
Generalization of findings, 3, 7, 26–27, 71, 85, 86, 87
General public. *See* Society

Global effects, 12, 81–83
Gross Domestic Product (GDP) implicit price deflator, 13, 24, 26, 34, 85

H

Head Start, xii, 5, 27, 85, 86, 87, 88, 90
    set of services, 88
Head Start Quality Research Consortium, xiii
Health benefits, 75
Higher education, 36–38
    assumptions about costs, 66–67
    estimated costs of, 37, 38
    gender differences for, 37, 38
High/Scope Educational Research Foundation, xiii, 19
High/Scope monographs, 4
High/Scope Perry Preschool program, 4, 15, 27. *See also* Cost of High/Scope Perry Preschool program
    analysis methodology, 6–16
    attrition, 4, 5, 25, 45
    bandwagon effects, 12, 82
    benefit-cost analysis of, 3, 65, 85
    benefit-cost ratio, xi, 85
    benefits of, xii, 9–10, 85, 86
    cost per child, 26, 85
    costs of, 8–10, 19–27, 85, 86
    costs to parents, 24
    curriculum, 4
    custodial care in, 27
    duration, 7, 8, 27, 88–89
    economic analysis of, 90
    economic return of, xi, 65, 85
    effect on crime reduction, 11, 50
    effect on earnings, 41 ff., 47
    effect on education, 11, 35–36, 45
    effect on education costs, 11, 28, 29, 34–35, 37–38, 66–67
    effect on employment, 11, 41 ff., 67
    effect on siblings, 10, 11–12, 75
    effect on welfare costs, 11, 58, 61–62
    evaluation of effects, 10–12
    experimental design of, 7, 71
    global effects, 12, 81–83
    as investment, xi, 65, 85
    long-term effects of, 3
    monetary value of effects, 12–13
    previous analyses, 4
    program quality, 4, 27, 88
    random assignment to, 5, 71, 72
    social environment for, 70–71
    staffing ratio, 4, 25, 88
    target population, 3, 5, 87
    teachers, 4, 26, 88
High/Scope Perry Preschool Project, 3, 4, 19, 82. *See also* High/Scope Perry Preschool program
Home ownership, 41, 49, 75
Human capital, 9

I

Implicit interest, 24, 25
Imputed interest, 23
Income. *See* Compensation, Earnings, Employment
Inflation, 13, 14, 15, 20, 24, 26, 85
Integrated special education, 30, 32, 33, 34
Internal Revenue Service, 23

J

Jury awards, 52
Justice system costs. *See* Crime costs

K

Kennedy, J. F., 91

L

Labor force participation, 41, 46, 74
Longitudinal data, 3

M

McDonald, M. S., 87
Marginal tax rate, 67
Marriage rate, 41
Medicaid, 58, 59, 60, 61
Michigan AFDC payments, 60
Michigan Public School Employees Retirement System, 20
Mixed-age grouping, 5
Monroe, E., 87

N

National Association for the Education of Young Children (NAEYC), 26
National Association of Securities Dealers Automated Quotation, 85
National Center for Education Statistics, 26, 37

National Center for Health Statistics, 45
National Victimization Survey, 52
Net present value, 15, 66, 69, 70, 77–81
New York Stock Exchange, 85
Nonmonetary effects estimates, 77–78
Nonpecuniary occupational benefits, 48
No-program group, 5. *See also* Study group
    arrest histories of, 51
    attrition, 45
    effect on earnings, 41, 42–43
    effect on education, 36–38, 42
    formal employment of, 67
    mother's employment at study entry, 5, 6, 71–72

O

Occupational status, 48
Office of Management and Budget, 14
Operating costs, 8, 20, 22, 31
Out-of-wedlock births, 75, 90

P

Panel Study on Income Dynamics, 60
Piagetian approach, 5
Preschool Intervention (Weikart), 19
Preschool programs, 87. *See also* Public policy, Public school prekindergarten programs
    changes in environment, 89
    duration of, 7–8, 27, 88, 89
Present value, 13, 14, 15. *See also* Net present value
Productivity growth, 46
Program group, 3, 5. *See also* Study group
    arrest histories of, 51
    attrition, 5, 6, 45
    benefits for, 9–10, 66, 69, 70, 77–81
    benefits to children of, 75
    costs borne by, 19, 24, 66–67
    costs and benefits for, 65–66
    educational outcomes of, 36–38, 42
    effect on earnings, 41, 42–43, 45–47
    formal employment of, 67
    gender differences, 6, 68, 69, 70, 74
    home ownership, 41
    labor force participation, 41
    marriage rates of, 41
    mother's employment at study entry, 5, 6, 71–72
    savings, 41
    siblings of, 5, 11
    socioeconomic status of, 5, 76
Program participants. *See* Program group
Psychological evaluation costs, elementary and secondary education, 30, 32
Public policy, 3, 26, 71, 82, 90
Public school prekindergarten programs, 5, 27, 87–89
Punitive damage awards, 52

Q

Queuing bias, 12, 82

R

Random assignment, 5, 71, 72
Randomized trials, 89
Reagan Administration, xiii
Real discount rate, 14–15
Real dollars, 13
Research, need for experimental, xiii, 69, 89, 90

S

Savings, 49
Schweinhart, Lawrence J., xiii, 4, 29
Sensitivity analysis, 6, 15–16, 65, 69–83
Social Security tax, 20, 48, 67
Social services, 58
Society, 73
    costs and benefits for, 15, 65–66, 67, 69, 70, 77–81
    net gain to, 3, 85
Socioeconomic status, 5, 76
Special-classroom special education, 30, 31, 33, 34
Special education, 29, 30, 82, 89
Speech-and-language support, 30, 32, 33, 34
Spillover effects, 12, 66, 82
Stanford-Binet IQ test, 5
Stock market, 85
Study group. *See also* No-program group, Program group
    attrition, 5, 6, 45
    benefits to, 15
    bias in, 6

comparison on variables at study entry, 5–6
educational costs of, 29
educational histories of, 28, 42
gender differences in, 6, 7, 8, 35
program duration for, 7–8
random assignment to, 5, 71, 72
sample size, 4, 7, 8
and siblings, 5, 11

T

Taxpayers, xii, 3, 15, 19, 73
 benefits to, 66, 67, 69, 70, 77–81, 85
 costs to, 9, 19, 66, 67, 69, 70, 77–81
Teachers, preschool, 26
Teacher salaries, 10, 21, 26, 27
Teen pregnancy, 75, 82, 90
Transfer payments, 53, 61, 67

U

Underestimation of benefits, 70
Uniform Crime Reports (Federal Bureau of Investigation), 55
U.S. Bureau of the Census, 28, 44, 46, 54, 85
U.S. Bureau of Economic Analysis, 24
U.S. Bureau of Justice Statistics, 51
U.S. Bureau of Labor Statistics, 26, 48, 67
U.S. General Accounting Office, 14

V

Victim costs. *See* Crime costs
Victimizations per arrest, 51

W

Weber, Carol, 19, 29
Weikart, D. P., 19
Welfare costs
 administrative costs, 61
 beyond age 27, 59–61
 estimated for program participants, 61
 gender differences in, 61
 preschool program effect on, 62
 projections for, 59–61
 reductions, 73
 through age 27, 58–59
 transfer payments, 53, 61, 67
Welfare dependency, 82, 86
Welfare effects, 11. *See also* Welfare costs
World Bank, xii
World War II, 46

Y

Ypsilanti, Michigan, 3, 5, 87
Ypsilanti Public School District, 4, 19, 21, 29, 87

About the Author

W. Steven Barnett is a professor of economics and policy in the Graduate School of Education at Rutgers — The State University of New Jersey. He received his Ph.D. in economics from the University of Michigan and has devoted his career to research on the economics of education and child development, with a special focus on children and families disadvantaged by poverty, disability, and discrimination. He has contributed to numerous journal articles and books on these and related topics, and he conducted a previous benefit-cost analysis of the High/Scope Perry Preschool program based on the data through age 19.